# TWENTIETH CENTURY VIEWS

The aim of this series is to present the best in contemporary critical opinion on major authors, providing a twentieth century perspective on their changing status in an era of profound revaluation.

Maynard Mack, *Series Editor*
Yale University

# GEORGE ORWELL

## A COLLECTION OF CRITICAL ESSAYS

Edited by

*Raymond Williams*

Prentice-Hall, Inc.  *Englewood Cliffs, N.J.*

A SPECTRUM BOOK

*Library of Congress Cataloging in Publication Data*

Williams, Raymond, comp.
  GEORGE ORWELL; A COLLECTION OF CRITICAL ESSAYS.

  (A Spectrum Book. Twentieth century views)
  Bibliography: p.
  1. Orwell, George, 1903–1950—Criticism and interpretation.
PR6029.R8Z865      828'.9'1209      74–11153
ISBN 0–13–647719–4
ISBN 0–13–647701–1 (pbk.)

10  9  8  7  6  5  4  3  2  1

PRENTICE-HALL INTERNATONAL, INC. (*London*)
PRENTICE-HALL OF AUSTRALIA PTY. LTD. (*Sydney*)
PRENTICE-HALL OF CANADA LTD. (*Toronto*)
PRENTICE-HALL OF INDIA PRIVATE LIMITED (*New Delhi*)
PRENTICE-HALL OF JAPAN, INC. (*Tokyo*)

Acknowledgment is gratefully made to the following for their permission to reprint quotations from the works of George Orwell:

To Harcourt Brace Jovanovich, Inc., Secker & Warburg, and Mrs. Sonia Brownell Orwell, for quotations from:

*Keep the Aspidistra Flying; The Road to Wigan Pier; Animal Farm; Looking Back on the Spanish War; Politics and the English Language.*

To Brandt & Brandt, Secker & Warburg, and Mrs. Sonia Brownell Orwell, for quotations from:

*Burmese Days* (Copyright 1934 by George Orwell. Copyright renewed 1962 by Sonia Pitt-Rivers).

*Coming Up for Air* (Copyright 1950 by Harcourt Brace Jovanovich, Inc.)

*Nineteen Eighty-Four* (Copyright 1941 by Harcourt Brace Jovanovich, Inc.)

*Down and Out in Paris and London* (Copyright 1933 by George Orwell. Copyright renewed 1960 by Sonia Pitt-Rivers)

# Contents

# GEORGE ORWELL

# Introduction

## by Raymond Williams

Most current studies of writing are studies of writers: conventionally isolated accounts of particular careers, achievements, and developments. The methodological criteria for such studies are thus to an important extent internal, as in this common formula: "We ask and answer only those questions that this writer's work requires us to ask." In practice this is often restrictive. What appears to be the rigor of critical discipline is often merely the rigor of a confined mind. For what is certain is that writing and writers vary, and that, therefore, the internal criteria for appropriate questions necessarily vary. Indeed, in some cases even the internal criteria indicate so wide an area of interest and question that our conventional notions of literature, and of the study of individual writers and works, come under severe pressure and finally break. In twentieth-century writing, there is no clearer instance of this than the writer we know as George Orwell.

Eric Arthur Blair (1903–50) began to write as George Orwell in 1933, the date of his first published book, *Down and Out in Paris and London*. Born in British-occupied India, he was educated in private schools in England and then became an officer in the Indian Imperial Police, serving mainly in Burma. He resigned this post in 1927 and spent several years trying to establish himself as a writer. During the 1930s he published four novels: *Burmese Days* (1934), *A Clergyman's Daughter* (1935), *Keep the Aspidistra Flying* (1936), and *Coming Up for Air* (1939). But he was better-known in this period for his reporting and journalism, represented in part by *The Road to Wigan Pier* (1937) and *Homage to Catalonia* (1938). From 1938 until his death he wrote several critical esssays on litera-

ture, popular culture, and politics and ideology. It is probably fair
to say that in the early '40s he was best-known for this work, and for
his reporting and journalism. In 1945 he published *Animal Farm,*
and gained a different and very much wider reputation. In 1949
he published *Nineteen Eighty-Four,* a book that not only confirmed
and extended his wider reputation, but made him part of the
climate of the age: a stimulus and a reference point in a period of
bitter political controversy. This controversy has continued un-
abated since his death in 1950, and one of its results has been that all
of his earlier work has been widely reprinted and extensively
studied.

It is thus obvious that the questions that Orwell's work requires
us to ask are not merely internal. There are important questions
about the method and substance of each of his books, and some
of them can be answered by the ordinary methods of literary study.
But all his books, equally, pose social and political questions, most
of them quite direct. *The Road to Wigan Pier* and *Inside the Whale*
lead us inevitably to questions about English society and politics,
and to more general questions about European and North American political thought and practice. *Homage to Catalonia* leads us
inevitably to the tangled and controversial history of the Spanish
Civil War. Even more remarkably, *Animal Farm* and *Nineteen
Eighty-Four* lead us inevitably to the controversial history of the
Russian revolution and its consequences, and to the politics of
the cold war; but because of this, they are more than merely books
that raise questions—indeed, they are themselves political events,
and the controversies surrounding them are part of our political
history.

There can thus be very little "pure" study of Orwell, although as
some forms of the political controversy have died down there have
been more formal literary studies of his earlier work and, increasingly, of even his late controversial books. Indeed, questions about
Orwell's practice as a writer seem inseparable from the political
controversy that attends his writing. Yet it can be said with some
certainty that whoever else might complain about the turbulent,
partisan, and wide-ranging controversy that has surrounded Orwell's

work, it would not be Orwell himself. Most of the ways in which he has been studied are the ways that he energetically practiced. Whether they are always satisfactory is another question.

## II

It soon became clear to me as I began to re-read the very considerable quantity of writing about Orwell that radical controversy was inevitable, and that the selection of the essays in this volume, however made, would itself be controversial. This is particularly true of the extraordinary body of writing about *Nineteen Eighty-Four*. I have in no way attempted to avoid this controversy, at either level. Yet it does seem to me that nearly a quarter-century after Orwell's death we might at least try to stop reading him backwards: that is, from the sensation of *Nineteen Eighty-Four* to the lesser-known earlier work. I therefore decided on a group of essays that in general follows the chronology of Orwell's development. This can be methodologically justified in the sense that we can then follow in detail and in nearly chronological order his practice as a writer. But there is a further justification. I believe that it was inevitable in the '50s that the political controversy surrounding *Nineteen Eighty-Four* should take precedence. The book was continually cited in public argument, and, with *Animal Farm*, became required reading in schools. Propaganda of every kind swirled around these two books and often incorporated them, making it difficult to determine whether they were themselves propaganda. That phase has not quite ended, but a generation now exists that has inherited and also examined the propaganda, and that has inherited and also examined the required reading. Above all it is this generation, at some distance from the original phenomena, that has insisted on studying Orwell's whole practice and development—reading the work as it evolved, reading it for its own sake and as a means of understanding what is now a distant sensation—and getting out of the habit of reading it backwards.

I can illustrate this from some of my own responses to the controversy. In 1956, a year of political crisis now remembered by the

names of Suez and Hungary, I wrote an essay on Orwell that became
a chapter of my book, *Culture and Society* (1958). A new world
was moving around us, and Orwell's significance, as I saw it, was not
in the *pro* and *anti* arguments that constituted the initial response
to *Nineteen Eighty-Four*. The generation of adults in the '30s—
who took positions about Soviet Communism and then exaggerated,
revised, or stuck to them through the Russian-German pact, the
Second World War, and the cold war—necessarily reacted to Orwell
as they would to one of themselves: as a liberator or a traitor; as a
truth-teller, simplifier, or slanderer. But Orwell was also the name
for the change of mind of this generation: a change of mind
that was seen as a hard-won and necessary truth, which must be
passed on intact to its successors. As recently as the late '60s, men
of this generation were still telling young political militants, who
in fact had absorbed the experience of that generation and had
set out on political courses quite different from it, to remember
their Orwell: not that a period had failed, but that a whole human
project had been shown to be fraudulent and, in its consequences,
cruel.

This was not how it seemed to me in 1956. Orwell was neither
traitor nor liberator, neither truth-teller nor slanderer. Rather,
very deep in his work were contradictions and paradoxes—including truth and falsehood, humanity and inhumanity—that he had
both articulated and been limited by, not only in his own remarkable development but also in regard to his generation as a whole.
I thus felt that a different kind of analysis was necessary and I developed this analysis in the aforementioned chapter in *Culture
and Society* in my book on Orwell in the *Modern Masters* series,
during which time fuller evidence and the lengthening historical
perspective seemed to confirm it. Meanwhile, a still younger generation, as I have indicated, was reading and studying Orwell as a
means of understanding the experiences of the '30s and '40s as a
historical sequence; this was very different from the first generation
of respondents, who, for example, had looked back from the "truth"
of the '40s to the "illusion" of the '30s—a contrast that most of their
successors were unable to share.

## III

I have thus arranged the essays in this volume so that Orwell's work may be studied in the general order in which it was written. I have included two of the earliest responses to the political controversy, the essays by Lionel Trilling and Isaac Deutscher. Most of the essays are from the generation immediately following, but I have deliberately included essays by Terry Eagleton, Stephen J. Greenblatt, and Jenni Calder, who represent a generation once again younger. Aside from the differences of tone and approach among the individual contributors to this volume, I believe that there are some significant differences among these three generations, differences that are particularly interesting in regard to Orwell.

Terry Eagleton's discussion of the novels is interesting for three reasons: first, because he considers the novels of the '30s seriously, within the recovered perspective of Orwell's whole work; secondly, because his critical analysis of these early novels is concerned with their developing internal tensions and contradictions, which are implicitly relevant to the later work; and third, because in the book from which his essay is taken, significantly entitled *Exiles and Emigrés*, Orwell is seen as part of the complicated development of a tendency in English culture, tracable to the time of H. G. Wells, which is summarized in Eagleton's analysis of the lower middle-class hero, a paradoxical and contradictory figure whose basic feelings and ideas can be interestingly related to Orwell's own position in the history of his time. In its close analysis of the elements of the novels, Eagleton's essay is a cooler and more distanced judgment than could have been written in any of the earlier decades.

A contrast in tone can be appreciated in the essay by Richard Hoggart, who was evidently closer to Orwell and who in his own book *The Uses of Literacy* was widely seen as developing some elements of Orwell's own work. There is of course some critical distance, and the tensions and contradictions in parts of *The Road to Wigan Pier* are carefully discussed. But there is also a strong and warm sense of Orwell as a colleague, a man whose voice would

belong in a contemporary argument. This is an important part of
the critical record: Orwell had and in some ways still has the power
of example and encouragement, even through disagreement. I can
recognize the same feeling of direct relationship to Orwell's life as
an example, in my own chapter in *Culture and Society,* and I
would not want to lose it. This feeling is different, not only from
Eagleton's analysis but from the position in a later brief piece of
my own, which I have included because I think the point it makes
about the relation between "documentary" and "imaginative" experience and writing follows from some of the difficulties in Orwell's
writing that Eagleton, Hoggart, and others have discussed, and
because this point about an overlap between documentary and
imaginative writing relates to a general problem that, in part because of Orwell's influence, has become more evident in British
and American writing of the '50s and '60s.

Lionel Trilling's essay on *Homage to Catalonia* is a classic statement of the general judgment of Orwell that shaped his initial
literary reputation: the man who told the truth. The case is better
put by Trilling than by anyone else that I have read. That it is
not only an important but an arguable case will be apparent from
parts of the essays that precede it. It also has special interest in its
relation to *Homage to Catalonia,* which, if Orwell's truth-telling
is to be taken as seriously as the conventional account insists, should
be read quite as often as *Animal Farm* and *Nineteen Eighty-Four.*
That it is not so read is an indication of the extent to which
Orwell's truth-telling was incorporated by official culture into truth-
telling against revolutionary socialism. Even in Trilling's account,
the disillusion with late Barcelona is given more emphasis than the
experience on which it depends: the rapturous discovery of and
commitment to Barcelona the revolutionary city.

E. P. Thompson's essay, which follows, is especially concerned
with analyzing the *kind* of disillusion that Orwell articulated and
that others learned from him. It is an important historical argument, significant in that it is part of Thompson's contribution to
a volume called *Out of Apathy,* one of the early manifestoes of the
British New Left. A complicated relationship with Orwell and
with the climate that incorporated him was a central feature of the

development of the British New Left, especially its first generation from 1956 to 1963.

John Wain (who has written several essays on Orwell) is much closer to Trilling's position. He has vigorously defended Orwell within the general terms of that interpretation. His own views and mine have clashed several times in the last ten years. However, I think his reading is important, and in its emphasis on Orwell's language (and incidentally, in its discussion of the critical essays) it is especially useful.

The next essay, by Stephen J. Greenblatt, is an interesting example of the more detached analysis of the most recent generation of critics. Greenblatt examines Orwell as satirist—his essay is from a study of three modern satirists. Some of his considerations are formal, and this is an effective way of discussing *Animal Farm*. Yet the essay is not simply formalist, and Greenblatt's interpretation of Orwell's persistent themes—in particular, his analysis of the "disillusion" of the '40s as a surfacing of the themes and tensions of Orwell's work of the '30s—is highly characteristic of the most recent mode of interpreting Orwell.

*Nineteen Eighty-Four* is often referred to in the preceding essays; in Greenblatt's it is explicitly considered. The two essays that follow are direct analyses of Orwell's last and most famous work, and were selected from an enormous body of writing about it. Isaac Deutscher's essay is the most considered political reply to *Nineteen Eighty-Four* and its orthodox reception. Written in 1954, it is understandably conscious of the political uses to which the novel was being put, and that argument remains important. But the essay is important also for a more academic reason: its tracing of Orwell's debt to Zamyatin's novel *We*. It is from the perspective of a longer and broader argument about revolution and its consequences that Deutscher, the leading revolutionary biographer of his generation, considers and in a sense puts down Orwell. The diagnosis of "disillusion" turning into the "mysticism of cruelty" is especially sharp.

It would have been easy to reprint one of the many replies to Deutscher within the terms of his original argument. But again I have chosen an essay from the most recent generation of critics. Jenni Calder's sustained discussion of the novel has the advantage, it seems to me, of the storm of argument that preceded her, and it is especially interesting to note the balance and discrimination that can thence be brought to bear on so disturbing and violent an original effect. Her discussion of Isaac Deutscher's essay is an obvious example of this, but it is true also of her more general analysis and assessment.

The selection concludes with two general retrospective essays. The short piece by Conor Cruise O'Brien is especially noteworthy because his combination of political and literary interests is as marked as Orwell's, and because his direct experience in international power politics, while at least as intense as Orwell's in Spain, is from a different generation. His relation of Orwell's English vision to the changed shape of the world of the '60s seems to me at once provocative and important. That altered international perspective is bound to have its effect on the way in which Orwell will be read in the future.

The essay by George Woodcock, which is taken from one of the best books on Orwell, is interesting as a sympathetic summation of his achievements and also for the specific points that the author makes about his use of language. It can be compared in this respect with John Wain's essay, and contrasted with, among others, those of Greenblatt and Hoggart. The argument about style and its relation to integrity is in one sense more characteristic of Orwell's period than of our own; the terms of literary analysis have in this respect shifted remarkably. Nevertheless, the modes and norms of Orwell's influential uses of language require precise and continuing study. The direct political legacy of his work, though still substantial, is inevitably diminishing. An Orwell writing in the '70s would not be dedicated to the intricate political conflicts of the '30s and '40s; involvement and contemporaneity are not abstract qualities but are, by definition, historically mobile and active. We can say that we ought to bring to the intricate and dangerous conflicts of our own times many of Orwell's qualities; his passionate involvement and integrity are the first that spring to mind. But that can never be the whole issue. One of Orwell's most powerful effects was a particular mode of attention to politics, and a mode of writing about it. It cannot be assumed that these modes are simply detachable and transferable; indeed, it may be that they are not part of the solution but part of the problem. It is especially in this area that useful further study of Orwell's work can be expected. The books and the career will continue to be studied, but the more general mode of discourse, not only by one writer but by a generation, will increasingly demand our attention.

# Orwell and the Lower-Middle-Class Novel

## by Terry Eagleton

✓*Burmese Days* is widely known as an assault upon Anglo-Burma, but what is less often remembered is its half-convinced apology, through the focus of the self-doubting Flory, for some of the regime's worst aspects. "Besides, you could forgive the Europeans a great deal of their bitterness. Living and working among Orientals would try the temper of a saint. . . . The life of the Anglo-Indian officials is not all jam. In comfortless camps, in sweltering offices, in gloomy dank bungalows smelling of dust and earth-oil, they earn, perhaps, the right to be a little disagreeable." "A little disagreeable," in the light of the brutal white-supremacy complex shown in the novel, seems something of an understatement; its real function is not so much to suggest a judicious "balance," but to half-ratify Flory's incapacity to formulate his own confused feelings into an explicit position, to validate his sense of impotent complicity with what he hates. (It is, significantly, the "atmosphere" rather than the political realities of imperialism he detests, a fact which itself implies a less than complete attitude and understanding.)

Flory veers between a frustrated raging at his compatriots (a feeling which the novel suggests is excessive and unfair) and what amounts to a declared cynicism. Neither attitude is really adequate; the first is too suggestive of the sort of committed moral judgement which can be achieved only by detaching oneself from a world of which one is part; the second, if consistently manifested, would make Flory no better than his fellow-countrymen. So the realities of

"Orwell and the Lower-Middle-Class Novel." From *Exiles and Emigrés*, by Terry Eagleton (London: Chatto and Windus, 1970), pp. 78–108. Reprinted by permission of Schocken Books, Inc., and Chatto and Windus Ltd.

Anglo-Burma can be neither totally accepted nor totally denied. On the one hand, there is this familiarly Orwellian outburst against the Deputy Commissioner:

> Nasty old bladder of lard! he thought, watching Mr. Macgregor up the road. How his bottom did stick out in those tight khaki shorts. Like one of those beastly middle-aged scoutmasters, homosexuals almost to a man, that you see photographs of in the illustrated papers. Dressing himself up in those ridiculous clothes and exposing his pudgy, dimpled knees, because it is the pukka sahib thing to take exercise before breakfast—disgusting!

It is the tone of outraged Orwellian decency: the shudder of the "normal" man, with his sober, puritan, self-consciously ordinary values, at "pansy" eccentricity of any kind; the tone of the criticism of the intellectual socialists and "Nancy poets" in *The Road to Wigan Pier,* replete with a tough, swaggering sense of self-righteous masculinity. It is not far removed from the kind of snobbish, physical disgust which characterises the racialist Ellis in *Burmese Days,* and its quality of *physical* repulsion is important: by virtue of it, an emotional rejection can be satisfied which does not press through, in other than a generalized sense, to an evaluation of the system which Macgregor symbolizes. On the other hand, because the feeling is unfocused and uncontrolled, missing the structure for the fragment of physical detail, it can turn, as easily, against Flory himself, in a callous self-deprecation which "realistically" undercuts the possibility of genuine criticism: "Seditious?" Flory said. "*I'm* not seditious. I don't want the Burmans to drive us out of this country. God forbid! I'm here to make money, like everyone else. All I object to is the slimy white man's burden humbug. The pukka sahib pose. It's so boring." This is intended to suggest a toughly attractive honesty—a rejection of colonial pretense, and so, to that degree, a moral superiority to others—at the same time as it binds Flory *to* those others, in his declared corruption of motive. It accepts the burden of guilt in order to avoid the contaminating risks of a moral stance—which would, presumably, be just one more form of "humbug." Flory must resist any suggestion that he is morally more sensitive or altruistic than others (even though, as the novel will show us, he clearly *is*) because this would be to take a stand on principle which his collusion with colonialism denies him, and so to live with the intolerable tension of bad faith. And so "honesty" and "pretense" are substituted, as moral alternatives, for good and bad.

The true corruption of imperialism, in fact, is that it denies the possibility of reliance on one's own "good" feelings:

> You see louts fresh from school kicking grey-haired servants. And the time comes when you burn with hatred of your own countrymen, when you long for a native rising to drown their Empire in blood. And in this there is nothing honourable, hardly even any sincerity. For, *au fond,* what do you care if the Indian Empire is a despotism, if Indians are bullied and exploited? You only care because the right of free speech is denied you. You are a creature of the despotism, a pukka sahib, tied tighter than a monk or a savage by an unbreakable system of tabus.

It is difficult to believe of the Flory we are actually shown that his anti-imperialist feelings are merely selfish; but the point, once more, is to qualify the possibilities of explicit commitment by insisting upon the "unbreakable" bond between moral judge and the situation judged, by seeing man as a puppet of his environment. The pattern of involvement and repulsion becomes a vicious circle: Flory is repelled by his own compromised involvement, and this is as much the source of his anger as any "objective" criticism of the colonialist system; yet the anger is in that sense egoistic—"You care only because the right of free speech is denied you"—and so is not to be trusted, lapsing back into a sullen acceptance of the *status quo.* Flory, one feels, is right to distrust his anger: the blurred, abstractly violent image of "drowning their Empire in blood" revealingly indicates its subjective quality. Yet the implication is then that considered moral judgments, which transcend an immediate condition and the raw response it evokes, are impossible. As in later Orwell novels, it is a choice between some vague, vicariously fulfilling image of apocalyptic destruction (the suppressed yearning for the bombs in *Coming Up for Air*), and the wry sense of "realistic" impotence which continually undermines it. Escape from being a creature of one's environment is possible through Romantic gestures or courageous moral commitments, and these cannot be wholly repudiated because they link one, in the midst of corruption, to one's "better self." Yet they are not only bound to fail, but also detach one from "normal" life into damaging moral isolation: "it is a corrupting thing to live one's real life in secret. One should live with the stream of life, not against it." To strike a radical stance in a conservative society is to risk the loss of identity, since identity is still located among the old, established customs and decencies, and Orwell could not trust to an idea of identity discovered through a *collective* rejection. And so Flory tells Dr. Veraswami that "You've got to be a pukka sahib or die, in this country." He criticizes the system—"if we are a civilizing influence, it's only to grab on a larger scale"—but from the vantage-point of an emotional and unarguable attachment to the old, primitive Burma which qualifies the value of his criticisms.

It is perhaps worth pointing out, at this stage, that there is a striking parallel between *Burmese Days* and Graham Greene's *The Heart of the Matter,* which is discussed in the following chapter. The resemblance lies not only in remarkable congruencies of setting and narrative detail—the seedy colonialist context, the machinations of a corrupt native leader, the arrival of a young English girl, the culminating suicide—but in the instructive parallels between Flory and Henry Scobie. Both Flory and Scobie are morally superior to their environments, yet both are corrupted by a guilty sense of collusion which narrows their awareness of what virtue they have, and so inhibits decisive moral action:

> "Cur, spineless cur," Flory was thinking to himself; without heat, however, for he was too accustomed to the thought. "Sneaking, idling, boozing, fornicating, soul-examining, self-pitying cur. All those fools at the Club, those dull louts to whom you are so pleased to think yourself superior—they are all better than you, every man of them. At least they are men in their oafish way. Not cowards, not liars. Not half-dead and rotting. But you—"

This self-castigation occurs after Flory has lacked courage to defend his Burmese friend before his compatriots; and it arises because the ethic of "honesty" turns against Flory himself. The racialists at the English club are at least "sincere," whereas Flory himself lives a deception. They may be "oafish," but they have at least a

sort of blunt, masculine integrity which Flory, with his ceaseless
"soul-examining," does not; they are "dull louts," but their dullness
renders them safely impervious to the "Nancy" poet style of self-
pitying introspection. It is here that Flory differs decisively from
Greene's Scobie. Scobie's self-castigation is intended to convince us,
negatively, of his unusual humility and so of his goodness; Flory,
who is much more directly a projection of the younger Orwell
himself, manifests his author's own guilty self-hatred and uncertainty. The men at the club are dull, but they are also (in a significant Orwellian epithet) "decent"; they may be bigoted and violent
but, the novel insists, they are not corrupted, wallowingly self-
indulgent, tremulously sensitive, like Flory himself. And part of
Orwell wants to affirm this judgement, to approve Flory's self-
disgust: a "tough," masculine honesty is once more stressed as superior to objective moral discriminations, to the point where a racialist is excused on the grounds of his sincerity. The choice is
between a dull, seedy world of "decent" normality, which can be
sworn at, mocked and caricatured but not wholly disapproved of,
and a sensitive, isolated self-examination which rides dangerously
near to the hated "Nancy" poets, picking over their own fine emotions. As with Wells's Mr. Polly, too much introspection is dangerous: it allows chaos to infiltrate and undermine the ordinary universe.

   *Burmese Days* is hesitant in its choice of these alternatives, and
its total attitude is correspondingly uncertain. There is, for instance, the problem of deciding precisely how much validity to
allow to Flory's introspections: the problem of steering a safe course
between unmanly sensitivity on the one hand and the straight
philistinism of Elizabeth Lackersteen or Verrall, the arrogant army
officer, on the other. The fluctuations of tone emerge in the following passage:

> Flory leaned over the gate. . . . Some lines from Gilbert came into
> his mind, a vulgar silly jingle but appropriate—something about
> "discoursing on your complicated state of mind." Gilbert was a
> gifted little skunk. Did all his trouble, then, simply boil down to
> that? Just complicated, unmanly whinings; poor-little-rich-girl stuff?
> . . . And if so, did that make it any more bearable? It is not the less

bitter because it is perhaps one's own fault, to see oneself drifting, rotting, in dishonour and horrible futility, and all the while knowing that somewhere within one there is the possibility of a decent human being.

Oh well, God save us from self-pity! Flory went back to the veranda. . . .

The jingle is "vulgar" and Gilbert is a "skunk"; but with these essential, distancing reservations safely made, the voice of English middle-class banality can be seriously attended to as appropriate. Once the significant status of Flory's experience has thus been denied, it is as quickly re-established in the following sentences, until the final gesture intervenes curtly to reconsolidate "common sense." The problem is really intractable: either Flory is to be taken seriously or he is not, and each possibility conflicts with an aspect of Orwell's intentions.

There are other ambiguities in the novel. It is difficult, for instance, to square Flory's sense of the manly integrity of his fellow-colonialists with his previous remarks to Dr. Veraswami about their self-deceptive pretentiousness; and it is generally difficult to accommodate Flory's forgiving estimations of them, in the light of his own guilt, to what we are shown of their actual brutality. One is forced to conclude that, when Orwell is actually presenting the men at the English club, he indulges his criticism to the full; but when the spotlight moves to Flory and his compatriots recede into the background, they gain a vicarious merit. The continuing conflict within Orwell's own mind, between an impulse to lonely and defiant moral gesture and a sense of the collective decency of drably normative life, goes unresolved. The first can find a vent for real criticism only at the cost of suggesting a corrupting self-indulgence and callow "ideologizing"; the second is admired for its ordinariness, its shrewdly realist refusal of large gestures, but cursed and hated for its petty sterility. In almost all of Orwell's novels, this dialectic hardens into deadlock: "ordinary" living is mocked and caricatured through the dehumanizing eye of a more intelligent observer, who is himself deflated—reduced to normality—by his own or others' scepticism.

When Flory first appears in the novel, our attention is drawn to

the disfiguring birthmark which stains his left cheek. The birthmark isolates him socially from others, marking him out as an
exile and even a freak; but it is also at the root of that sensitivity
which emerges, especially in his doomed relationship with Elizabeth Lackersteen, as his most admirable quality. The birthmark
is connected both with his sensitivity and with his habit of passive
compromise:

> Meanwhile, Flory had signed a public insult to his friend. He had
> done it for the same reason as he had done a thousand such things
> in his life; because he lacked the small spark of courage that was
> needed to refuse. For, of course, he could have refused if he had
> chosen; and equally, of course, refusal would have meant a row!
> The nagging, the jeers! At the very thought of it he flinched; he
> could feel his birthmark palpable on his cheek, and something hap-
> pened in his throat that made his voice go flat and guilty.

Flory, who has carried his disfigurement through years of schoolboy
taunts, is a victim, not just of Anglo-Burma, but of life; and the
upshot of this is to contribute to the ambivalence with which he is
characterized. On the one hand, this agonized awareness of his
ugliness half-excuses his compromise: the responsibility for his
failure to act by moral principle began, not with him, but "in his
mother's womb." So in this respect, the birthmark is a telling detail
which the novel can mobilize in support of its thesis that moral
stances are impracticable. By selecting a hero stamped from birth
with the insignia of failure and hypersensitivity, it suggests that
Flory's weakness is in the "nature of things" rather than in his
response to a particular moral situation. But the birthmark also
makes Flory nontypical, estranged at the outset from "normal" human life: Elizabeth comes finally to hate him "as she would have
hated a leper or a lunatic." So the scar dignifies Flory, lending him
a compassion superior to others, but only at the cost of implying
that he—and men like him—are really "half-men"—freaks. And
this, again, is detrimental to the validity of his criticisms of others.
It is a choice between the "normal," insensitive man—Verrall and
his kind—and the lonely eccentric. There is no suggestion that a
"normal" man could take up the critical position which Flory assumes: his criticism is a function of his isolation, his desperate

need to be understood, which is in turn a function of his bachelor-hood, and that of his disfigurement. The novel certainly goes a good way towards endorsing Flory's raging at imperialism; but it suggests, simultaneously, that the anger is privately motivated, the gesture of a man who is out of the ordinary, and to that extent not a reliably "objective" critic of the system. It is finally the birthmark, and not differences of ideology, which seems to Elizabeth her main reason for rejecting Flory: "It was, finally, the birthmark that had damned him." The two elements (the birthmark and ideological conflict) are, of course, closely interrelated in Flory's history; but the fact that the genetic issue finally predominates over the social question seems to throw the burden of Flory's tragedy, not on to his moral and political conflicts with his fellow-countrymen, but on to what he physically and unchangeably is.

In this and in other ways, *Burmese Days* is really less a considered critique of imperialism than an exploration of private guilt, incommunicable loneliness and loss of identity for which Burma becomes at points little more than a setting. The pain which Flory suffers is "the pain of exile"; but because that exile, by virtue of the birthmark, goes "deeper" than social causes, criticism of the imperialist system is again tempered by a sense of overriding futility. Flory's view, common enough in Orwell, that political stances are merely temperamental rationalizations, is more or less endorsed, to the ultimate detriment of the novel's moral judgements. Despite its obvious political context, *Burmese Days,* in comparison with other of Orwell's novels, is perhaps the least directly social: what really occupies its center is the personal relationship of Flory and Elizabeth. (It is worth adding that for this reason the novel succeeds technically more than most of the others, precisely because it avoids that direct confrontation with a social condition which in later works leads to a crude and latently unbalanced generalizing. It also succeeds because Orwell, like Flory, loves Burma as much as he hates it, a fact which reveals itself in the rich precision of physical description (the landscape, the leopard-hunt), and which disappears when Orwell shifts his attention to England, which cannot, as a physical place, be loved at all.

In the case of Flory, then, we have Orwell's earliest working of tensions and contradictions which remained painfully unresolved throughout his career as a writer. Flory can neither accept, nor disengage from, the "normality" of a hated social system; he can refuse complicity with some of its worst aspects, but only at the cost of a compromised cynicism which reveals him as a "half-man," a soulful and self-pitying outcast. His incapacity for decisive action works in his favor, when it is set against the arrogant certainty of a Verrall; yet this ineffectuality is also his major flaw. If he were more determinedly anti-imperialist, he would see Elizabeth Lackersteen for the callous prig she is; his inability to see this is not only exasperating in a man so sensitive to such callousness in others, but reveals the extent to which he himself shares colonialist feelings, leading him to excuse her desertion of him for Verrall. "What right had he to be jealous? He had offered himself to a girl who was too young and pretty for him, and she had turned him down —rightly." Elizabeth's behaviour has, in fact, little "right" about it; but Flory can only be allowed to recognise this at the risk of self-pity. So, once more, the effort to avoid the risks of introspection leads straight into a condonement of arrogantly colonialist behavior. There is no alternative between a full-blooded condemnation of imperialism which would involve the deceptions of self-pity and of a committed moral stance, and a rejection of self-pity, an acknowledgement of one's own complicity, which more than once blunts the edge of the criticism that part of Orwell wants to make.

If what is at stake in *Burmese Days* is an incapacity either to accept or transcend the texture of "normal" social existence, the same can be said of Orwell's next novel, *A Clergyman's Daughter*. The novel's structure is very simple: Dorothy Hare, a rector's daughter devoted to the small duties of the parochial round, loses her memory, undergoes the experience of the Orwellian underworld (hop-picking, destitution, school-teaching), and finally returns to the rectory to continue her old life. She is rescued from the underworld life by Warburton, a middle-aged bohemian roué who wants to marry her; and the novel's crisis (in so far as it has one, given its rambling, social-documentary structure) is Dorothy's rejection of his offer. What Warburton offers her is essentially a kind of hedonist escape from the deadening trivia of the small-town parish; but

although Dorothy has learnt the emptiness of this world from her
London experience, and to this extent transcended its crippling
limits by losing her Christian faith, an escape must be refused:

> The point is that all the beliefs I had are gone, and I've nothing to
> put in their place.

Warburton, the emancipated aesthete, is willing to accept and live
with this lack of meaning; but Dorothy, while rejecting provincial
life intellectually, is still emotionally committed to its values of
work, duty, usefulness, decency: in a word, to its conformist "normality," despite its newly revealed vacuousness. Experience and belief have proved to be incompatible; but Dorothy, while unable
any longer to accept a belief which thrived simply on an ignorance
of social experience, is also unable to accept a life of experience as
an end in itself.

Because of this inability, the jovial generosity of Warburton
comes to seem tainted, fickle, amoral: when he tries to kiss Dorothy
she sees him suddenly as a "fat, debauched bachelor." The physical
revulsion is again significant: it is really a way of simplifying the
argument, in a typically Orwellian device, by linking despised
moral positions to physical obscenity:

> She was in the arms of a man—a fattish, oldish man! A wave of dis-
> gust and deadly fear went through her, and her entrails seemed to
> shrink and freeze. His thick male body was pressing her backwards
> and downwards, his large, pink face, smooth, but to her eyes old, was
> bearing down upon her own. The harsh odour of maleness forced
> itself into her nostrils.

Dorothy's sexual frigidity has previously been the target of the
novel's satire: it has signified her pious Anglican innocence. But
now, in a sudden shift, it is used in her favor against Warburton:
the virginity which the novel has emphasized as a narrowness, in its
first chapters, is now enlisted in a campaign against the pressures of
worldly, free-thinking emancipation. The life of the rectory is
deadly and drab, but the escape which the Dickensian Christmas
figure of Warburton offers must be rejected:

> When he put his arm around her it was as though he were protecting
> her, sheltering her, drawing her away from the brink of grey, deadly

poverty and back to the world of friendly and desirable things—to
security and ease, to comely houses and good clothes, to books and
friends and flowers, to summer days and distant lands.

These alternatives must be denied, because the grey and deadly
world, although empty and stifling, is at least *real:* it is where most
people have to live, and escape is false and privileged. It is a conflict of the puritan virtues against the hedonist, and although
Dorothy has undergone an experience which confirms Warburton's
nihilism and casts the puritan virtues into radical question, the alternatives are Romantic and unthinkable. The full consequences
of her experience cannot be faced, for there is no middle ground
between narrow devotion and emancipated flippancy. Dorothy can
no longer accept her world, but neither can she reject it; the movement to freedom and renewal, here as in all of Orwell's novels,
ends in failure. Life is hopeless and sterile, but the worst false
consciousness is to think you can change it.

Dorothy is acutely aware that what she has lost, in abandoning
Christian faith, is a "totalization": a whole structure which can
render experience intelligible, linking its smallest parochial details
to a general understanding. Once this has broken under the weight
of experience, no other totalization is conceivable: "There was, she
saw clearly, no possible substitute for faith; no pagan acceptance of
life as sufficient to itself, no pantheistic cheer-up stuff, no pseudo-
religion of 'progress' with visions of glittering Utopias and ant-
heaps of steel and concrete." She is left, simply, with the amorphous
chaos of experience, which is both inferior to such totalizations in
that it is meaningless, but superior in that it is "real." Finally, she
discovers a sort of refuge in the empirical facts of experience themselves: the solution to her difficulty emerges as the stock Victorian
response of "get(ting) on with the job that lies to hand." And so
the gently satirized attitude she had when the novel began—the
brisk, spinsterish, self-sacrificial attention to minute tasks—is ultimately affirmed, as superior to a radical criticism of contemporary
life which could only be, like Warburton's, that of the "Nancy"
poets: decadent, self-indulgent, eccentric and in a sense indecent.
Dorothy has changed, but only in consciousness: "It is the things
that happen in your heart that matter." And although Warburton's

view of life is to that extent endorsed, his belief that it can be acted on is by the same token dismissed. Warburton, in fact, is a curious blend of generous wisdom and hard-boiled philandering—partly a Cheeryble, partly a Micawber or Skimpole—and both attitudes are essential: the first is a necessary criticism of Dorothy's way of life; the second heavily qualifies such criticism and so validates the escape back to the rectory. The inescapable implication is that a rejection of ordinary experience is bound to be unprincipled; yet the alternative is not that the common life is to be gladly embraced. On the contrary, the novel's way of seeing that life has from the outset connived at Warburton's distaste for human society: this characteristically Orwellian description of one of the Rector's parishioners, for instance:

> In her ancient, bloodless face her mouth was surprisingly large, loose and wet. The underlip, pendulous with age, slobbered forward, exposing a strip of gum and a row of false teeth as yellow as the keys of an old piano. On the upper lip was a fringe of dark, dewy moustache. . . .

Ordinary experience is physically disgusting, but the disgust must be painfully overcome, as Dorothy conquers her repugnance at rubbing embrocation into an old lady's legs. It is just that any articulate formulation of this repugnance, such as Warburton makes, must be inhibited by the pressure of guilt: the feeling that the "grey, dead" life, however obscene, is where one really belongs.

Dorothy, then, escapes from the limiting perspectives of the rectory into an underground world of broader experience; yet what she gains from that broadening is ambiguous. On the one hand, it must be enough to expose the unreal pieties of the rectory, to allow access to the true emptiness of reality; yet on the other hand it must not be permitted to subvert too deeply a commitment to that life to which she can return. Part of the novel's technique for sustaining this balance is to be found in the process by which Dorothy enters and inhabits the world of hop-picking and vagrancy. Somehow, the novel has to introduce her into this sphere other than by her own conscious decision: for such a decision would not only be mysteriously obscure in the light of her previous, respectably devotional existence, but would also signify the sort of definitive critical rejection of that existence from which extrication back into the rectory would prove difficult. So the novel selects the simple, improbable device of translating Dorothy from the Suffolk rectory to the back-streets of London by a sudden loss of memory, silently eliding the physical process which this dramatic transition involves. Once Dorothy is immersed in this confused amnesiac state, two concomitant problems can be overcome. First, because she moves in a "dazed, witless" trance, a "contented and unreflecting state," the question of adequate motivation for her unlikely behavior in travelling with petty criminals to Kent can be suspended; she can, as it were, undergo the whole "underground" experience of the younger Orwell himself without our questioning the probability of this in terms of her pious and spinsterly temperament. More importantly, by avoiding the *conscious* critical choice which directed Orwell's own callowly Romantic "low-life" explorations, Dorothy is not required to question her previous history in a way which would cause difficulties over her final return to it. The loss-of-memory gambit simply effects a neat transition from rectory to common lodging-house without raising the complicated issues of motive and purpose which, as a *conscious* process, this would inevitably involve.

Secondly, because of the amnesia, the whole episode takes on the quality of a dream. In this state, "You act and plan and suffer, and yet all the while it is as though everything were a little out of focus, a little unreal." Dorothy is a sort of automaton, moving with uncritical and unreflective contentment in a world of grotesquely unfamiliar experience. The consequence of this is to diminish the solid significance of what experience she has, in a way which allows her final return to the rectory to appear as a re-assumption of "normal" life after an interim and unaccountable suspension of it. There is, in other words, a genuine though submerged question in the novel about the status of her underworld adventures: is this the "reality" which the small Suffolk town deceptively concealed, or is it an unreal interpolation, a salutary but eccentric fantasy? It is the question we put to the novelist who stands behind much of Orwell's work and who is detectable in some of the characterizations of this book: is Fagin, or Brownlow, "real" life?

There is a sense in which the novel wants to assert both attitudes at once. It is essential that the underworld should be sufficiently "real" to disclose the lying pretensions of bourgeois normality; yet the alternatives to that normality, whether "above" it, in the cosmopolitanism of Warburton, or "below" it, in the world of tramps and prostitutes, must at the same time be exposed as in some sense "unreal": as unreliably untypical diversions from the ordinary universe. And so Warburton is presented as two-dimensional, and the criminal underworld assumes a quality of fantasy, through the befuddled mind of Dorothy. Because of that befuddlement, she is able to "experience" the broader world, but without reflecting critically upon it; it is noticeable that we are nowhere shown her actual responses to her adventures, but allowed to see her only from the outside. And so the final conclusions she draws are restricted: she has learnt from the underworld the unreality of ordinary life, but only because she has also seen the emptiness of the wider life, which is thus not in any sense an alternative. Like Flory, she is caught between an overwhelming sense of the falsity of contemporary society and a consciousness of the dangers involved in formulating that sense into anything which might resemble a "position."

Orwell's pre-war development, from *Burmese Days* and *A Clergyman's Daughter* to *Keep the Aspidistra Flying* and *Coming Up For Air*, reflects his movement towards an increasingly explicit, more frontal engagement with the tensions which preoccupied him; but it registers, for related reasons, an accelerating artistic decline. As the central dilemmas become less oblique and more urgently intractable, the treatment becomes significantly cruder, the impulse to violent, cursing caricature and uncontrolled loathing progressively less resistible. As the pressures of a disintegrating society, moving quickly to the brink of war, are increasingly taken, the qualities which distinguished *Burmese Days* and even parts of the notably inferior *A Clergyman's Daughter*—the acute sense of physically active life, the shrewd feeling for social detail—become over-whelmed by a generalizing rhetoric. The sense of social reality is still alive in the childhood scenes of *Coming Up For Air*; but it has taken the form of rambling, unstructured social-documentary ob-servation which cannot be significantly related in feeling or quality to contemporary life.

One index of this growing loss of control is the changed relation between author and protagonist: the degree of objectivity possible in the presentation of Flory or Dorothy dwindles damagingly in the later instances of Gordon Comstock and George Bowling. This is not, of course, to suggest that Comstock, in *Keep the Aspidistra Flying*, is uncritically characterized: rather that what is critized in him is essentially what Orwell criticizes in himself, and that in this respect he does not cease to be a too-direct projection of his au-thor's own confused and unachieved attitudes. Gordon's dogmatic rejection of capitalism for an underworld existence is seen as im-possibly histrionic—"The poet starving in a garret—but starving, somehow, not uncomfortably—that was his vision of himself"—yet his modes of feeling are nevertheless strongly endorsed. Comstock's dehumanizing perception is essentially Orwell's: "The pink doll-faces of upper-class women gazed at him through the car window. Bloody nit-witted lapdogs. Pampered bitches dozing on their chains. Better the lone wolf than the cringing dog." In this way, the novel's criticism of its hero is a regulative factor: it allows Orwell to in-dulge his own less intelligent feelings under the cover of critical detachment from them. The self-pity which was generally avoided in the case of Flory is now either directly unleashed ("It was the feeling of helplessness . . . of being set aside, ignored—a creature not worth worrying about"), or sidestepped only in a way which is really just a more subtle form of the same emotion, coated with a desperate "realism": "He was thirty, moth-eaten, and without charm. Why should any girl ever look at him again?"

By virtue of Gordon's belief that money is the all-determining factor in every human feeling and relationship, the novel is able to maintain the tension between a criticism of the formal, ordinary world and a criticism of attempts to escape it. If the ordinary world is corrupted by money, then a committed stance against it will also be financially undermined. So commitment will fail absurdly, but not in a way which reflects any particular credit on the established society. Moreover, once Gordon's money-doctrine is accepted, we are persuaded to half-excuse his more self-indulgent behavior—his callous treatment of his girl-friend Rosemary, for example—because lack of money becomes a covering formula for all types of weakness: "Social failure, artistic failure, sexual failure—they are all the same. And lack of money is at the bottom of them all." In believing this, Gordon is holding an attitude which merely reflects the views of the bourgeois world: he is, in this respect, thoroughly endorsing bourgeois values, bound to the world he rejects by a simple inversion. Gordon rejects middle-class society from what are essentially middle-class premises: his extraordinary sensitivity to such matters as the social significance of kinds of doorbell indicates the depth of his obsession with the insignia of a social structure he is supposed to reject. The important point is that Gordon, in subscribing to a financial estimation of human qualities ("No woman ever judges a man by anything except his income"), dehumanizes men as thoroughly as does the society he assaults. He would dismiss the view that, even within the corruptions of capitalism, men are still men, and their relationships can still partially transcend the crude determinants which limit them, as "unrealistic" humanitarianism; and the novel, at least at points, would seem to confirm his attitude. Like Orwell himself, Gordon oscillates between Romantic gesture and a cynical accommodation to the *status quo,* seeing no other possible standpoint; like Orwell, he is anti-Romantic in the way that only a confirmed Romantic can be.

It is significant, in the light of the choices offered in the novel, that Gordon's ideological opponent is not an experienced working-class socialist, but Ravelston, the rich, guilty, middle-class left winger. The result is a typically Orwellian conflict between the amorphous complexities of sordid "experience" on the one hand and the abstract rigidities of "ideology" on the other. "Ravelston . . . knew . . . that life under a decaying capitalism is deathly and meaningless. But this knowledge was only theoretical. You can't really *feel* that kind of thing when your income is eight hundred a year." Gordon's "front-line" defense against socialism, then, is an appeal to the immovable misery of his own life; but his "second-line" defense is a cynical acknowledgement, in the manner of Flory, that his arguments are in any case only the arbitrary projections of private feeling. He attacks Ravelston's socialist argument, but then, in a second move, detaches himself cynically from his own scepticism:

> "All this about Socialism and Capitalism and the state of the modern world and God knows what. I don't give a —— for the state of the modern world. If the whole of England was starving except myself and the people I care about, I wouldn't give a damn."
> "Don't you exaggerate just a little?"
> "No. All this talk we make—we're only objectifying our own feelings. It's all dictated by what we've got in our pockets. . . ."

Gordon is forced to deny the validity of his own experience, since even this leads him towards a (purely negative) "position"; in order to express the full quality of his cynicism he must at the same time negate it by suggesting that it is, after all, purely subjective and so valueless. He is, of course, correct—his pessimism *is* a subjective projection—yet at the same time the novel's own way of looking works to suggest an at least partial endorsement of the view that "It's all dictated by what we've got in our pockets." The novel is thus vulnerable to a serious criticism: in order to affirm the validity of Gordon's dramatic rejection of society, it must show his evaluation to be objectively true; but in order to protect both itself and its hero from the dangers of declared moral commitment, it must at the same time deny the objective validity of the position it takes. The uncertainty registers itself, once more, in a fluctuation of attitude within the text:

> He gazed out at the graceless streets. At this moment it seemed to him that in a street like this, in a town like this, every life that is lived must be meaningless and intolerable. The sense of disintegration, of decay, that is endemic in our time, was strong upon him. Somehow it was mixed up with the ad-posters opposite. . . . Corner Table grins at you, seemingly optimistic, with a flash of false teeth. But what is behind the grin? Desolation, emptiness, prophecies of doom. . . . The great death-wish of the modern world. Suicide pacts.

> Heads stuck in gas-ovens in lonely maisonettes. French letters and
> Amen pills. . . . It is all written in Corner Table's face.

The vision of meaninglessness begins as Gordon's own: this is how
it "seemed to him," and the novel does not rush instantly to confirm his view. His attitude belongs to the decay of the times, which
lends it more solid substantiation but still leaves it open to question. Then, as the passage gathers speed, it is no longer clear
whether the speaking voice is Comstock's or Orwell's: what began
as a character's attitude is generalized to an image of society which
seems, in the dogmatism of the final sentence, to have been finally
established as "objective."

Similar ambiguities can be found throughout the book. Gordon's
stance is revealed as deliberately self-indulgent—"He clung with a
sort of painful joy to the notion that because he was poor everyone must *want* to insult him"—yet, equally, the significance of his
experience seems confirmed: "He perceived that it is quite impossible to explain to any rich person, even to anyone so decent as
Ravelston, the essential bloodiness of poverty." There can, in other
words, be no traffic between the raw stuff of experience and the
categories of understanding and analysis; like Flory, Gordon insists
on the inherent incommunicability of his deprivation, the impossibility of ever being understood, as a way of avoiding an articulate
formulation of his experience which might involve him in a "commitment"—to changing the society, for instance. The experience
remains jealously private, a mode of defiant self-definition against
the world. This attitude is certainly criticized; but because Gordon's poverty is real, a critic of his behavior is placed, for lack of
an alternative standpoint, in the shoes of Ravelston. He can risk
criticism of Gordon's attitudes only at the cost of a damaging charge
of patrician remoteness from the realities of Gordon's existence.

The choice which the novel poses, then, is essentially that defined
by Flory in *Burmese Days*: one must either be a pukka sahib or
die. "Serve the money-god or go under: there is no other rule."
It is a sharper choice than that in *A Clergyman's Daughter*, where
the belief still lingered that an external accommodation to society
could be made in a way which preserved an interior consciousness

from its falsehoods. In *Aspidistra* this posture is much less viable: if attitudes are so mechanically determined by economic environment (and Gordon's belief is that kind of vulgarization of Marxism), then there can be no balanced compromise. Gordon must finally re-enter society, impelled, significantly, by the forces of "decency." That decency is embodied both in Ravelston (who throughout the novel symbolizes one side of Orwell as Gordon symbolizes another: the generous, wryly "realist" compromiser as against the self-indulgent Romantic), and also in Rosemary, who is to bear Gordon's child. The money-god cannot be fought "when he gets at you through your sense of decency"; the struggle between the impulse to determined moral commitment and the undermining claims of a weary "common sense" is decided in favor of the latter.

Yet it is not decided without considerable ambiguity. Gordon's return to society suggests the impracticality of his venture into a social limbo without, however, too radically questioning the validity of that venture. It also indicates the inevitability of a return to routine social life without implying either that this is a sort of betrayal or that it is deeply valuable. Gordon's plan has been to sink low enough in the social structure to free himself from bourgeois claims: "Down in the safe soft womb of earth, where there is no getting of jobs or losing of jobs, no relatives or friends to plague you, no hope, fear, ambition, honour, duty. . . . That was where he wished to be." It is a way of negating the whole range of common drives and feelings without particularly having to act: a passive subsiding into social death, into the fertile darkness at the base of society. This, as Ravelston points out, is a "mistake": one can't live in a corrupt society and escape corruption. Yet it is not particularly suggested that this mode of "social" protest is inherently inadequate: a capitulation rather than a constructive challenge; a selfishly individualist rather than a collective transcendence; a false idealizing of those at the end of the social scale who seem to Gordon most free from oppression but who are in reality most deeply exploited. It is merely suggested that such a gesture might be possible for saints, but not for Gordon.

On the one hand, the return to lower middle-class life is seen as a compromise (Gordon will "sell his soul" to his firm); but it is also seen, suddenly, as a return to "decent, fully human life," in a way which is difficult to square with the descriptions of that life elsewhere in the novel:

> He wondered about the people in houses like this. They would be, for example, small clerks, shop-assistants, commercial travellers, insurance touts, tram conductors. Did *they* know that they were only puppets dancing when money pulled the strings? You bet they didn't. And if they did, what would they care? They were too busy being born, being married, begetting, working, dying. It mightn't be a bad thing, if you could manage it, to feel yourself one of them, one of the ruck of men. Our civilisation is founded on greed and fear, but in the lives of common men the greed and fear are mysteriously transmuted into something nobler. The lower middle-class people in there, behind their lace curtains, with their children and their scraps of furniture and their aspidistras—they lived by the money-code, sure enough, and yet they contrived to keep their decency. The money-code as they interpreted it was not merely cynical and hoggish. They had their standards, their inviolable points of honour. They "kept themselves respectable"—kept the aspidistra flying. Besides, they were *alive*. They were bound up in the bundle of life. They begot children, which is what the saints and the soul-savers never by any chance do.

The transitions of attitude here are interesting. "Ordinary" life is still seen externally, as a kind of curiosity, and the physical setting of the meditation (Gordon is looking at a street of houses) powerfully underlines the sense of a distanced analysis of the inscrutable. People are still "puppets," and the observer thus distinguished from them by his superior insight; yet if one could plunge into the ruck of men, in a movement at once self-conscious and self-abnegating, one might perhaps find value in their lives. The lower middle class are still dehumanizingly described—notice the casual equivalence of status between lace curtains, children and furniture—but they are, at least, "decent," and even in some nebulous sense "alive." We have not previously seen "life" and "respectability" as equivalents, but now we are asked to do so, as a way of ratifying Gordon's return. So the novel finally perceives the humanity which remains at the heart of capitalism, but chiefly, one feels, as a kind of afterthought, a tactic for rendering Gordon's surrender acceptable.

Moreover, the sense of nobility in the common life is not allowed
to override, even at this point, the more typically negative feelings
towards it which have run throughout the novel, the patronizing
Orwellian contempt for the "little" men: "He would be a law-abiding little cit like any other law-abiding little cit—a soldier in the
strap-hanging army. Probably it was better so." Is it "better so"
because Gordon has no other choice (he feels "as though some force
outside him were pushing him"), and is thus acquitted of responsibility? Or because a denial of society, although morally admirable, is simply impractical? Or because society is, after all, of value?
It is something of all of these: but the shifts of attitude obscure the
issue, trying to salvage the value of social rejection while simultaneously affirming the merit of social settlement. (We do not, for instance, know how much Gordon has lost by his abandonment of
poetry, and so how truly detrimental his re-integration might be,
since neither we nor he can decide whether he is a good poet or a
bad one.) Orwell remains ambiguously stranded between two positions: once more, an intensely emotional rejection of the decent
aspidistra world clashes head-on with a sense of pragmatic decency
which rejects such intense emotions as privileged luxury.

Orwell's next novel, *Coming Up For Air,* represents, not an extension, but a re-working of the problems we have examined so far.
It is his most typical "lower middle-class" novel, obsessed with the
cheapness of "suburbia," permeated by a tired, cursing, ragged de-
featism and underpinned by a semi-hysterical sense of anxiety and
estrangement as war approaches. The choice of the first-person nar-
rator, George Bowling, is itself significant. Bowling is fat, seedy
and disillusioned, an integral part of the decaying suburban world
he criticizes, yet imbued with a quality of ironic insight superior
to those who surround him. There is thus, from the outset, no possibility of the experience offered by the novel being "objectively"
appraised—not only because no other character is allowed to advance an opposing viewpoint, but because Bowling's disgust with
his environment is qualified by a cynically devaluing sense of his
own corruption, his inert complicity in the world he despises:

> Don't mistake me. I'm not trying to put myself over as a kind of
> tender flower, the aching heart behind the smiling face and so forth.

> You couldn't get on in the insurance business if you were anything like that. I'm vulgar, I'm insensitive, and I fit in with my environment. . . . But also I've got something else inside me, chiefly a hangover from the past. . . . I'm fat, but I'm thin inside. Has it ever struck you that there's a thin man inside every fat man, just as they say there's a statue inside every block of stone?

Bowling, an "ordinary, middling chap," fits in with his environment: but neither so thoroughly that he cannot achieve a reflectively critical standpoint towards it, nor so loosely that he can analyze it as a whole and imagine an alternative. Through the focus of Bowling, then, the novel is able to project a criticism of society which is the more convincing because it emerges, not from the contemptible "abstractions" of the ideologists, but from a man trapped within its limits. Yet by the same token, the criticism cannot be "positive," since Bowling's title to criticize without arrogance or abstraction is gained from the fact that he bears around the seediness he discerns within his own grotesque physique. He is superior in insight to others, but not too much so:

> The usual crowd that you can hardly fight your way through was streaming up the pavement, all of them with that insane fixed expression on their faces that people have in London streets. . . . I felt as if I was the only person awake in a city of sleep-walkers. That's an illusion, of course. When you walk through a crowd of strangers it's next to impossible not to imagine that they're all waxworks, but probably they're thinking just the same about you.

The point of this is both to affirm and to qualify his greater perceptiveness: to allow him a partial transcendence of his environment without the deceptions of disengagement. In one sense, Bowling is presented with a greater degree of objectivity than Gordon Comstock: he is a vulgar, philandering philistine, and is seen by the novel to be so. Yet, as with Comstock, the point of this distancing is to permit Orwell to indulge his own cruder feelings—his malicious delight in cruel parody, his own sporadically philistine contempt for intellectuals, his gushingly apocalyptic despair, his desire for destructive violence—while at the same time protecting himself, by virtue of his spokesman's seedy grossness, from any direct commitment to these attitudes.

The qualities which give Bowling a right to be heard, then, are
also the qualities which prevent him from achieving any meaningful organization of his experience. The world dramatized through
his eyes is fragmented and unreal: the synthetic frankfurter he swal-
lows early in the novel symbolizes an insubstantial world where
everything is "slick and streamlined, everything made out of something else." The most interesting point at issue is not the stock
quality of this judgement: whatever local force it might have looks
less impressive when it is placed in the context of Bowling's per-
vasively jaundiced world-view, his monotonously one-dimensional
perception of his environment. The significant point is that, here
as in other novels, this feeling of social unreality conflicts with an
opposing sense of the inert solidity of the suburban world. Bowling's perception of his society is colored by the insistent thought
of impending war: he is struck by the strangeness of the notion that
the routine world of London, its houses and factories, is likely to
be brought into destructive collision with an abstract world of political strategy and theory. He imagines "bloomers soaked in blood"
on a washing-line, disturbed by this connection of the domestically
known and the abstractly feared. And this works both ways: to
sharpen a sense of the indestructible *reality* of the experienced social world ("Miles and miles of streets, fried-fish shops, tin chapels,
picture houses . . .") in contrast to the intangible forces of international politics; but also to highlight the fragile unreality of the
quotidian, its vulnerability to destruction. The question, once
again, is which world is more "real." Bowling recoils from suburbia, but satirizes Porteous, his intellectual friend, for his aesthetic
escapism. On the other hand, little of the same satire attaches to
Bowling's own escapist and ill-fated return to Lower Binfield, his
childhood home.

The ambiguity emerges most sharply in the account of the political meeting which Bowling attends in Part Three of the novel.
The anti-Fascist speaker is made to seem a purveyor of mindless,
ranting hatred; yet the fear of Fascism he articulates is also Bowling's own, and Bowling can therefore equally satirize those in the
audience who cannot understand the lecture. Both commitment and

apathy are despicable: Bowling's shifts of feeling towards the audience register the contradiction:

> So perhaps after all there *is* a significance in this mingy little crowd that'll turn out on a winter night to listen to a lecture of this kind. Or at any rate in the five or six who can grasp what it's all about. They're simply the outposts of an enormous army. They're the long-sighted ones, the first rats to spot that the ship is sinking. Quick, quick! The Fascists are coming! Spanners ready, boys! Smash others or they'll smash you. So terrified of the future that we're jumping straight into it like a rabbit diving down a boa-constrictor's throat.

The audience is "mingy," but is grudgingly allowed a significance —a significance limited in the next breath to the few, like Bowling himself, who can understand, and which thus preserves intact a dismissive attitude towards the rest. The image of the "long-sighted ones" then defines that importance, but the following image—that of the rats leaving the ship—instantly curtails any suggestion of active virtue. Then, with the following, hysterical phrases ("The Fascists are coming . . ."), a fear which is in fact Bowling's most characteristic feeling is detached from himself and projected on to the audience, as a way of distancing himself from their, and his own, involvements. It is only the "we" of the final sentence which acknowledges (lest Bowling be given too much lonely moral distinction) that this is a common condition in which he himself is implicated. Once more, Orwell's novel embodies a paradox: those who escape from the ordinary world by intellectual pursuits or political ideologies are satirized, but so also are those who involve themselves "mindlessly" with it. The only viable stance is one of passive withdrawal *within* the world: the Bowling posture, midway between fool and intellectual, law-abiding "cit" and radical ideologist, stupefied masses and contemptible capitalists, "Progress" and "Culture." It is the classical stance of the lower middle-class hero.

# Introduction to *The Road to Wigan Pier*

## *by Richard Hoggart*

This book has been disliked by almost all commentators on Orwell. Tom Hopkinson calls it his worst book and Laurence Brander "his most disappointing performance." Disappointment began when the typescript reached the desk of its publisher Victor Gollancz who had commissioned the essay. It duly appeared in 1937 but with a preface in which Mr. Gollancz, though doing his best to be fair and to appreciate fully what he had been offered, showed his disagreement on every page.

He had good reason to be surprised, for this must be one of the oddest responses to a commission which even the Left Book Club inspired. The club was intended to mobilize and nourish socialist thought. With his co-editors John Strachey and Harold Laski, Mr. Gollancz issued each month to club members, under the imprint of his own publishing house but in distinctive limp orange covers, a book designed to help these ends. He had asked George Orwell to write a "condition of England" book, a documentary on the state of the unemployed in the North, a book of descriptive social analysis. What he got was a book in two equal halves, neither of them what he had asked for. Part I seems to be roughly on the contracted subject but approaches it most idiosyncratically. Part II is partly cultural autobiography, partly opinionation about socialism by a man who had then a patchy idea of the nature of socialism.

The truth was that socialism was at that time fairly new to Orwell, and *Wigan Pier* was his first directly political book. Nor was he much known, so that the club editors were to some extent

"Introduction to *The Road to Wigan Pier*," by Richard Hoggart (London: Heinemann Educational Books, 1965). Reprinted by permission of the publisher.

chancing their collective arm. Orwell had published his first book, *Down and Out in Paris and London* (social observation but not directly political writing), four years before. He had followed it at yearly intervals with three novels, all interesting but the first probably the best (*Burmese Days, A Clergyman's Daughter, Keep the Aspidistra Flying*). When the Gollancz commission came he was living in Essex, keeping a village store and writing. He threw up the shop to go north for this book. But there was no great financial loss, if any; the shop produced only £1 a week and up to the age of thirty-seven Orwell, so he used to say, never earned more than £3 a week from his writings. He did not go back to the Essex shop. After handing over the typescript of *Wigan Pier* he set out for Spain to enlist on the Government side (but characteristically chose to serve with the militia of a minority group on the extreme left). The relentless enquiry which had led him from filthy work in Paris kitchens to London dosshouses and the Brookers's tripe-shop-cum-boarding-house finally brought him to the front near Huesca where, luckily for him, he got a bullet in the neck and so eventually came home.

It was not a pilgrimage for which anything in Orwell's background gave a prior hint. He was born Eric Blair (the "Orwell" came from a river near which he once lived in Suffolk) into the upper classes. With his characteristic effort at precision in matters of class Orwell called himself in this book a member of "the lower upper middle classes." His point was that his father was a public servant, not a landowner nor a big businessman; so, though he had the rank, status and tastes of a gentleman, his salary was modest. He was, in fact, a minor official in the Indian Customs service and George was born in Bengal, in 1903. He was, as was usual, sent to a preparatory school in England, a school which he described with great bitterness in the essay "Such, such were the joys." From there he won a scholarship to Eton which he also wrote about, though with less bitterness. When the time came to leave Eton Orwell was unsure of his plans and in particular unsure about whether or not he should try to go to Cambridge. A tutor, with what reasons we do not certainly know, suggested that he should

take a job abroad. Orwell joined the Indian Imperial Police and
served for five years (1922–7) in Burma. In some respects the central character of *Burmese Days*, Flory, is Orwell himself.

It is plain, from *Wigan Pier* as well as from many of Orwell's
other writings, that he was reacting intensely against his social and
educational background, was much of the time trying to cast off
his class. But he always respected certain characteristic virtues of
his class, such as fairmindedness and responsibility. And it is worth
remarking at this early point that in some deep-seated ways Orwell
was himself characteristic of his class and (though he was an acute
analyst) didn't always realize how much this was so himself. To
begin with, he had a kind of fastidiousness (which is not the same
as gentility) which never deserted him and which much of the time
he was fighting. But it was there. It was reinforced by his phenom-
enally sharp sense of smell; he could *smell* his way through complex
experiences. Thus, he tells us in this book that at first he found the
English working-classes physically repulsive, much more repellent
than Orientals. Look, too, at a tiny but characteristic moment in
this book. He constantly drove himself into extreme and unpleasant
situations and could describe them with exactness. One of the best
passages in *Wigan Pier* is the description of the nature of work
down the mine. It is terribly hard and grimy work, and Orwell
wanted his readers to know this. In the course of his description he
says that he suddenly put his hand on "a dreadful slimy thing
among the coal dust." Orwell uses that word "dreadful" frequently
and usually means something really inspiring horror. So one wonders what it will prove to be this time. It is in fact a quid of chewed
tobacco spat out of a miner's mouth. Not a particularly pleasant
thing to put your hand on; but, for a man who had deliberately
subjected himself to the trials and squalors which Orwell had,
hardly a "dreadful" thing, one would have thought. So the phrase
unintentionally acts as a sudden shifter of perspective: used in that
way, it comes straight out of the vocabulary of the class which Orwell's journeys were a way of escaping from. Inevitably, in describing this little incident in full (but one could hardly make the
point otherwise) I have given it too much weight. It is a small
pointer but an accurate one to a quality that Orwell never lost and

which was partly (but not wholly; he was also *by nature* fastidious) socially acquired.

At other times (and this quality can be seen in Part II of *Wigam Pier* and most notably in the essay "England Your England") Orwell revealed a particular kind of toughness in manner, a sort of anti-intellectual pugnacity which reminds you of a no-nonsense upper-class colonel. This from a man who could a few chapters before talk so warmly and gently about working-class interiors. The two characteristics do not blend: they remain throughout Orwell's short life (he died in 1950) a contradictory mixture.

More important, to this tracing of Orwell's deep-seated connections with his class, he was one of the latest in a long and characteristic English line: those dissidents which a system that is in so many ways designed to reproduce its own kind has always managed to produce richly. In this aspect of his character Orwell joins hands, among men of this century, with Lawrence of Arabia. They went in different directions, geographically and intellectually; but in their tempers they had much in common.

All these tensions finally brought Orwell out of the Indian Imperial Police and sent him on the first phase of his journey to the lower depths. He had to go, of that there is no doubt. But why? There are easy answers and hard answers to this question, and all probably have some truth in them. But to establish anything like a satisfactory *order* of reasons would require a much fuller study of Orwell—not only of his works but of his life—than we have had so far (or than we are likely to have if his wishes are respected, since he asked that there should be no biography).

In trying to touch bottom, Orwell most obviously was reacting against imperialism and against his own guilt as a former agent of imperialism. He came to regard it as evil. Not just because one side was a tyrant to the other: not all the British rulers were tyrannical, and Orwell was as likely to dislike a Buddhist priest as a British colonial policeman. He believed that imperialism was evil because it distorted the moral character of both the oppressor and the oppressed.

So when he came back to an England in the grip of a slump, with millions unemployed and therefore many more millions *directly*

affected by unemployment, he felt that he knew what he had to do.
He had to associate himself with the oppressed half of England
rather than with his own kind by birth and training. He had to
feel for himself the pressures the poor felt and suffer them; he had
to get to know the victims of injustice, had to "become one of
them." He had to try to root out the class-sense within himself. He
did not have a romantic idea of what that last duty meant; he knew
it always means trying to root out a part of yourself.

But that explanation, though it contains some of the truth, is
not the whole. The whole truth is more varied. To touch bottom
for Orwell was a very complicated release indeed, a shedding of
guilt but also a positive test to which he was impelled. Phrases like
the following occur throughout his work and are typical of an important characteristic of the Orwellian stance: "it had to be done,"
"there was nothing else for it," "it is a kind of duty." They are
brave phrases and have a grandeur; they are also the phrases of a
very vulnerable man and an obsessively *driven* man, a man with
at times a burning sacrificial egoism. As so often with writers, Orwell's use of language, the words and images he instinctively chose,
show this more quickly and surely than his actual statements. Describing his first trip to the rock-bottom poor, the fear and then the
relief when a down-and-out lumbered straight at him—and then
embraced him and offered him a cup of tea, he says: "I had a cup
of tea. It was a kind of baptism." It is the image which stands out.

By nature Orwell was a lonely man. He wanted to belong to a
coherent society, he longed for a sense of communion. But he could
never quite believe in the eventual good effect of any man-made
groups. "No one who feels deeply about literature, or even prefers
good English to bad, can accept the discipline of a political party,"
he said in his introduction to the first volume of *British Pam-
phleteers* which he edited with Reginald Reynolds. He could just
as characteristically have said, "No one who feels deeply about *life*
. . . can accept . . ." In an interesting chapter of *Culture and Society* Raymond Williams discusses Orwell's representative importance as a modern intellectual, representative of "the dissociation
between the individual and society which is our deepest crisis." The
argument is interesting and subtle and should be read. But this

condition may well be, as Mr. Williams recognizes, as much a matter of individual temperament as of the climate of the age; Orwell's attitude was at least as much personal as representative.

It may be that, more deeply than he knew (and this is ironic since he so much distrusted intellectuals who did not belong), Orwell was temperamentally a lonely, isolated intellectual. He was always seeking out the lepers of life, yet he shrank instinctively from physical contact. Critics of Orwell who are committed to a creed will of course carry their interpretation of Orwell's "metaphysical loneliness" further. In his full-length study of Orwell Mr. Christopher Hollis, who is a Roman Catholic, sees him as a deeply religious man who, for reasons both temperamental and cultural, could not accept any religion; sees him as a believer without a religion, a man full of convictions, full not only of a moral sense but of metaphysical assumptions (hence—without them in the background—his convictions, to Mr. Hollis, would be meaningless).

Certainly the passion behind much of Orwell's feeling was inspired by a very un-material sense of man; and at key moments his language often moved into the metaphors of religion. This can be seen in the baptism image just quoted. Just before Gordon Comstock and Rosemary, in *Keep the Aspidistra Flying,* decide to marry rather than get rid of their unborn child by abortion Orwell says, of Gordon: "He knew it was a dreadful thing they were contemplating—a blasphemy, if the word had any meaning." In its image and in its doubling back upon itself at the end that sentence nicely catches the "religious" feeling of Orwell and the dry metaphysical unexpectancy. He was an intensely moral man. He knew in his bones, to quote a phrase he accurately described as evidence of the natural religion of many working-class people, that we are "here for a purpose." But he could settle in no church and with no formal religion.

Though he found membership of organized groups difficult Orwell had an exceptionally strong feeling that we are members one of another, that we belong to each other, that all men are brothers. No one ever needed to remind Orwell that he should not send to find for whom the bell tolls; he knew. That was partly why he went to Spain and the other places. During the war, it is said, he

and his first wife deliberately went short on their rations (Orwell
thought this hastened his wife's death) so that there would be more
for other people. The remarkable fact here is not that they went
short; others did that. But most went short so as to help someone
*known* to be in need, someone identified—an old lady down the
road or a local hospital. The Orwells went short so that there would
be "more for others," and this is both a saintly and an intensely
familial act. It conceives the whole nation as one family. It doesn't
calculate or assume that if you let yourself go short some official will
make away with what you have saved, or someone else down the
road will waste it anyway, so why bother. Orwell had a rooted sense
of Britain as a family, as a continuing community (he was, to use
one of his own distinctions, a patriot but not a nationalist). "England is a family with the wrong members in control," he said in an
epigram which neatly catches his attitude: it assumes that we are a
family, and it grumbles about the way the family is being run. This
doubleness is itself very much a family attitude, a basic acceptance
and a readiness to criticize in a way we would not be happy to accept from outsiders.

These impulses seem to have been moving the man who set out
north to fulfil Victor Gollancz's commission. No wonder the result
was a surprise. The North of England was stranger to Orwell than
Burma. Not only had he spent many years out of England; he was
by class and domicile apart from the heavy industrial areas of the
North. They hit him hard, and the harder because he saw them at
the worst time, at the bottom of the slump. He set out to re-create
as vividly and concretely as he could the shock of this world of
slag heaps and rotting basements, of shabby men with grey clothes
and grey faces, and women looking like grandmothers but holding
small babies—*their* babies, all of them with the air of bundles of
old clothes roughly tied up, the world of the Means Test and of
graduates nearly penniless and canvassing for newspaper sales. This
is the thirties all right, for many in the working-classes a long-
drawn-out waste and misery which only the preparations for the
war of 1939 ended. Whatever the qualifications we make to Orwell's account we would falsify our own history if we tried to qual-

ify it out of existence. These things happened not long ago in this country (as they are happening in many other countries now); and it matters greatly—matters, as Orwell would have been the first to admit, far more than simply the need to get *his* record right—that we should take their emotional measure.

The qualifications are many and critics have not spared them. Orwell, as John Beavan points out, picked out the most depressed of the working-classes. The respectable working-class hardly appear in his pages. He chose the miners and, more, the unemployed miners. He chose also people on Public Assistance, the unemployable and the shabbily itinerant, the kind of people who land up at the Brookers'.

All these qualifications are true. So is the charge that Orwell sometimes sentimentalizes working-class life. His famous description of a working-class interior *is* slightly idealized and "poetic." His account of the working-class attitude to education is oversimplified, and given a touch of the noble savage.

Before we look more closely at these charges we could add some others which are not so evident. Orwell's picture of working-class life, even of that good side typified in a working-class interor, is too static, is set like a picture caught at a certain moment. So it becomes in part a nostalgic looking back (and for Orwell himself probably also suggested an un-anxious calm, free of status-striving, which was a balm to him). In general his portrayal of the working-classes in *Wigan Pier* has not sufficient perkiness and resilience, is a bit dispirited. One can see why, given the kinds of people he chose to describe. Still, he did offer it as a picture of "the working-class." Later, in his last full-length work *1984* (in all but this a terrifyingly hopeless novel), Orwell was to say "if there is hope it lies in the proles." But from the "proles" of *Wigan Pier* we would not get much hope of resistance and rebirth. There is just a hint now and again of a related quality, the ability to soldier on, to stick together and bear it, that basic stoicism which Orwell himself possessed and which may have been one of the reasons why he found the disposition of working-class people so immediately attractive.

When all has been said Orwell's picture, though not the whole truth, was truer than almost all the other documentary material

which came out of the documentary thirties. It was true to the
*spirit* of its place and time and (with the reservations noted) its
people. It was true to the spirit of the misery:

> and this is where it all led—to labyrinthine slums and dark back
> kitchens with sickly, ageing people creeping round and round them
> like black beetles. It is a kind of duty to see and smell such places
> now and again, especially smell them, lest you should forget that they
> exist; though perhaps it is better not to stay there too long.

Orwell's picture was true too to the spirit of some of the good
qualities in this environment. He was not foolish when he said
that he felt inferior to a coal-miner, though he has been called so;
within the terms defined in that first part of *Wigan Pier* he was
talking humane good sense then. He may have sometimes senti-
mentalized working-class interiors. But fundamentally he is not
wrong to praise working-class interiors. It demanded, especially
then, a special sort of insight and hold on truth to be able to speak
about the "sane and comely" home life those interiors represented.
And it is not at all foolish—as some have called it—it is sensible
and humane, to say that the memory of working-class interiors
"reminds me that our age has not been altogether a bad one to
live in."

It is important to be sure of our own motives here. Some writers
on Orwell, sympathetic though they are to much of his work, have
tried to shuffle off this side because it makes them uncomfortable.
But he knew what he was about. It is no accident that again and
again in this book he directly addressed himself to people of his
own class. The "old ladies living in retirement at Brighton" are
representative figures for a great many more, for politicians and
businessmen and writers and *rentiers* and university lecturers. It
was to these above all that Orwell was speaking. He was trying to
correct that conveniently distant vision of other people's problems,
that face-saving view of slum life and slum dwellers, which the
training of his class offered him; he was insisting that people *do*
hate living in slums (remember the sight of a young woman poking
at a blocked waste pipe which printed itself on his memory as the
train carried him south again), that even if some have become so

dispirited as not to seem to mind, or have adapted themselves, it is still rotten—rotten for them and rotten for what it does to the souls of those of us who are willing to let other people live like that. These attitudes die hard and they are not dead yet.

In the beginning of its second half *Wigan Pier* is autobiographical about the sense of class. Inevitably, Orwell has been accused of exaggerating, of carrying on wars already long dead. He did exaggerate now and again; this was rough polemical writing. But it is important to say firmly that Orwell's sense of the importance and the pervasiveness of class in Britain was sound, sounder than that of most of those who criticize him for it. He feels the smallness of small snobbery accurately. He grasps the rooted nature of class feeling and the immense effort needed to grow out of it. He knew (as many people today still do not recognize) that it cannot be got rid of with a smile, or by calling a garage mechanic "Charlie." To believe that it can is one of the continuing self-deceptions of the British. Orwell was right to stress the subtle pervasive force of class, the way in which it cuts across and sometimes surmounts economic facts.

The professedly socialist parts of the book which follow are not so easily defended. The comic-grotesque gallery of cranks whom Orwell attacked—pacifists, feminists, fruit juice drinkers, quakers, birth control fanatics, vegetarians, nature cure quacks, nudists, and "nancy poets"—these were to him the left-wing intelligentsia, the literary intellectuals and the middle-class socialists. Towards them all he was intemperately violent.

Of course, there is some truth in what he says. A man with Orwell's insight could not fail to score some shrewd hits. But at bottom his attack was probably inspired as much as anything by his puritanical mistrust of self-indulgence, physical or mental. His great antagonism to the left-wing intelligentsia was founded in his feeling that they were intellectually and imaginatively self-indulgent. He sombrely hated what seemed to him moral shallowness. He thought them prim and out of touch with decent ordinary life. He thought they wanted to have things both ways, to get socialism on the cheap whilst remaining undisturbed in their own fundamental attitudes and habits. He thought they wanted to remain

dominative or at least distantly paternal in their attitude towards
the workers rather than to recognize the need for a radical change
of outlook. In his view, they thought they could remain vaguely
international in their socialism without facing the full implications of their beliefs (which Orwell had proved in action he *was*
ready to face). They thought they could be true socialists and yet
keep their prosperity, though that was founded on the subjection
of millions of colored people; "we all live by robbing the Asiatic
coolies." For Orwell, responsibility, responsibility in action, existed
all the time, was heavy and had to be obeyed.

All this is useful. But Orwell did not leave it there. He was
grossly unfair to his victims. At one moment he was asserting that
working-class habits are better than middle-class and seemed to be
mocking the middle-classes and urging them to drop their middle-
class habits. At another moment he was warning them not to dare
to try. At yet another time he was telling them that they cannot
drop their middle-class habits anyway because they are too in-
grained. At still another time he said that he could not drop middle-
class habits himself. It is a confused, harsh and one-sided attack
and omits altogether the history of good and self-forgetful action
which many middle-class socialists have shown. On the other hand,
Orwell idealized some working-class socialists and omitted to criticize—it would have been easy to do so—the limitations of, for example, some professional trade-unionist politicians.

More than all this, his attack purported to be an attack on the
main body of socialists. As such it is fantastically inadequate in
scope. The left-wing intelligentsia are only a small part of the
Labor movement (though a valuable part). Outside them there is
a complicated range of other people and groups: unions, co-opera-
tives, local branches, chapels, friendly societies and the like. All
these and many other groups and individuals make up the texture
of British socialism.

Something similar could be said about Orwell's attack on machine
society which also runs through this part of the book. He had a
continuing fierce suspicion of the emergence of a beehive state, a
rage which later lay behind his two most famous books—*Animal
Farm,* where it was controlled as an apparently light-hearted alle-

gory, and *1984* in which it erupted into terror (but by then Orwell
was a sick and indeed dying man). His tirades in *Wigan Pier,*
though sometimes pointed, have nothing like the edge and force
of D. H. Lawrence's. One may often agree with him because one
has long accepted the particular point (without being clear what
next can be done about it), but Orwell did not often illuminate
the issues. Here, as in some other places, one has to be on guard
not to be carried away by him. He had such an *honest* voice, as
we all say; he so often said, outright, things we have all wanted
to say and have been inhibited from saying, that we are in danger
of being swept away. We have sometimes to distinguish between
sentimentality and hysteria on the one hand and a just rage and
pity on the other.

This book more than any other of Orwell's shows a host of contradictions in his thinking—between an absolutist and a tolerantly
gentle man; between a resilient man, out to get things done by
communal political action, and a dark despairer; between one who
urged the need for revolutionary changes in our thinking and a
man with a deep-seated sense that things would always go on much
as they always had ("every revolutionary opinion draws part of its
strength from a secret conviction that nothing can be changed,"
he says in this book; and elsewhere: "on balance life is suffering,
and only the very young or the very foolish imagine otherwise");
between a pessimist and an optimist who believed in the eventual
triumph of ordinary good sense. These things came together in his
interest in working-class people. His pity for their condition made
him want to bring about change for them; his basic, stoical acceptance and unexpectancy made him—with one part of himself—
not really believe in the efficacy of change and made him also admire, with a peculiarly close natural feeling, the *stillness* of working-class interiors. It is probably useful to follow a reading of *Wigan
Pier* with *Homage to Catalonia,* in which Orwell describes his experiences in the Spanish Civil War. This is a much more variously
spirited book and much surer of itself. By then some of the things
so far unproved for Orwell at the time of *Wigan Pier,* especially
about his capacity to live up to his own convictions, had been
proved.

There is a danger at this point of making *Wigan Pier* sound too faulty, too unfinished to be worth much attention. This would be a serious mistake. It has some impressive parts and is, as a whole, unforgettable. When we are trying to explain this we usually say that it is because of Orwell's exceptional honesty. What does "honesty" mean here? And is honesty in itself enough to make a memorable writer, whatever it may imply for a man as a man? I think that honesty here means a certain way of seeing, and the possession of the power of showing what it is you have seen. It means a certain manner and *quality* of perception, and a style which isolates it. It means an eye for telling gesture and incident—for instance, the ability to notice that the mine's offices had a rubber stamp which said simply "death stoppages." Reading that, you know unforgettably how much the risk of death is accepted in mining. It means the sense of detail and verisimilitude which allowed Orwell to create atmosphere in much the same way as Defoe and Cobbett. We do not easily forget the exact description of the "fillers'" work at the coal face, or the budget of a family on PAC, or the "scrambling for the coal" on the slag-heaps, or Mr. Brooker's dirty thumb finding its way into everything.

We mean also by Orwell's "honesty" his training himself to get rid as far as possible of the expected, the social-class, response. You can almost feel him disciplining himself to the point at which, when he looks up and says "what different universes different people inhabit," such an obvious remark seems to have the fresh validity of a self-forged truth. He tests on himself, bites between his teeth, the kind of socially conventional coinage which most of us merely accept; he tests it by talking flat out about the smell of working-class people or about assumed differences in status and the misery they cause.

All this seems a down-to-earth common sense though it is in fact so uncommon as to be a form of high intelligence. The total effect, which is why we use the word "honesty" so often, is as though we saw the thing, the scene, the incident as though for the first time.[1]

[1] Two particularly effective short pieces in this kind are "A Hanging" and "Shooting an Elephant" (George Orwell, *Collected Essays*, Secker and Warburg, 1961).

To be able to write like this was partly due to natural gifts, partly to deliberate professional practice (Orwell always meant to be a writer); and partly it is the product of a moral tension. It is informed by an urgent, nonconforming and humane personality.

To embody this outlook Orwell forged his peculiar style. It is, at first glance, clear and neutral, one of the least literary or involuted or aesthetic (one of Orwell's bad words) styles. "Good prose is like a windowpane," he said, and set about stripping his down. Like Yeats, Orwell thought there was "more enterprise in walking naked." His style was a function of his search for truth. He thought of it as a weapon, a political weapon (which is not the same as a *party* political weapon); "I have been forced into becoming a pamphleteer," he said in "Why I Write." He was in no doubt about the importance of language in this respect, as we may easily see from his essay on "Politics and the English Language" and even more from his invention of Newspeak in *1984*. But his sense of the relations between language, thought and imagination was sometimes superficial.

The style Orwell forged was direct, active, cogent and epigrammatic. It rarely qualifies; it has not many "perhapses" or "somewhats" or "rathers" or "probables" or "sort of" or "on the whole." It uses short and ungenteel words wherever possible and says "bum" instead of "behind" or "belly" instead of "stomach." It is directed at a "you" outside, who has to be convinced; when Orwell is impassioned the "you's" succeed one another like an indictment. It is demonstrative—"Here is this frightful business of . . ." and "One of those ready-made steak puddings . . ." It gives the reader a feeling of relief because it refuses to pussyfoot. It says "This swindle . . ." and you feel firm ground under your feet. It has a distinctive kick and energy. One critic, Richard Rees, calls it "debonair." This is not the word that would come first to mind, but when you think about it you realize that it is true and helpful, since it reduces the risk of talking about Orwell's style as though it were only that of a plain honest George.

When Orwell was moved his style lifted to match his feeling and the reader himself feels as though he is confronting experience rawly and nakedly. Look, for instance, at the opening page of this book. There is the short direct placing paragraph referring to the mill-girls' clogs and factory whistles and then we are straight into the description of the Brookers' lodging house. Notice especially how the epithets and images all work to build up a particularly loathsome impression. They are thrown at the reader, like blows with a wet dish cloth. The opening of E. M. Forster's *A Passage to India* makes an interesting comparison, not so as to award comparative marks but to see how far Orwell had gone in removing the "civilized" modulations, the literary and "read" air, from his style so as to arrive at an immediate and demotic voice:

> Except for the Marabar Caves—and they are twenty miles off—the city of Chandrapore presents nothing extraordinary. Edged rather than washed by the river Ganges, it trails for a couple of miles along the bank, scarcely distinguishable from the rubbish it deposits so freely. There are no bathing-steps on the river front, as the Ganges happens not to be holy here; indeed there is no river front, and the bazaars shut out the wide and shifting panorama of the stream.

At its best this voice of Orwell's is charitable, morally earnest and convincing. At its worst, it can deceive us by the misuse of just those qualities which elsewhere make its strength. The apparently clear run of the prose can, like that of Matthew Arnold's at times, be deceptive. Orwell can commit, and commits in the second part of *Wigan Pier,* most of the faults he attacks in others. He can write loosely and in cliché. Very soon after the opening of the second part of this book he is writing about the "dreary wastes of Kensington," of their inhabitants as "vaguely embittered" and of their "favourite haunts." He overuses certain words for quick effects, words such as "frightful," "dreadful," "awful" and "evil-smelling." He sometimes overcharges his metaphors and this is usually a sign of emotional looseness. After talking about the evils of imperialism with a man from the Educational Service he had met on the train, he says in this book: "In the haggard morning light when the train crawled into Mandalay we parted as guiltily as any adulterous couple." Some of his larger generalizations only slip by us at a quick reading because he has built up a reputation with us as an honest broker; on a closer reading we find that the invoice has been

incorrectly made out. He uses limiting labels as a form of Instant
Insult; there are plenty of examples of this in *Wigan Pier*.

So it is easy to see why some people are suspicious of Orwell, and
why those of us who are drawn to him need to be on our guard so
as not to be seduced by his manner in itself. I use that curious
choice of words deliberately because Orwell was one of those writers
who gives the reader a particularly strong sense of himself as a
man. His personality is inextricably intertwined with his writing;
his life and art were mutually complementary political acts, in the
larger than usual sense I defined above. As Lionel Trilling says, he
belongs to that group of writers who *are* what they write.

He always drove himself hard and no doubt hastened his death,
at the age of 47, by forcing himself to finish *1984* whilst living on
the damp and remote island of Jura. For all the apparent straight-
ness of his manner he was, as we have seen, a peculiarly complex
and ambiguous man. No doubt all of us are complex and ambiguous, but Orwell differed both in the strength of his ambiguity
and in the fact that he expressed it in his life and in his writing
at the same time (and with less than the usual artistic indirection).
He was tolerant, generous, brave, charitable and compassionate;
he was also irritable, fierce, bitter, and indignant (but not "right-
euosly indignant" in the self-righteous sense). He was at one and
the same time sceptical and sentimental, conservative and radical,
unideological and intensely moralistic (this is a specially English
combination), insular and internationally-minded, austere and full
of fellow-feeling.

Orwell has often been called "the conscience of his generation."
Alexander Trocchi, whilst agreeing in general, added that the
"conscience" of a generation is not the "consciousness" of a generation but a less penetrating, because too immediately committed,
entity, one too much tied to political action here and now. Similarly, Tom Hopkinson argues that Orwell suffered because he was
"without historical perspective" and adds that this gave him the
peculiar intensity of his attention to matters of the present day.
One can agree so far here—whilst reflecting that Orwell himself
might have said that some kinds of "historical perspective" can
make us lose all sense of urgency and intensity in working for

reform, so that we more easily accept the inevitability of misery.

But there is truth in both these criticisms and they do help to define Orwell's limits. To call Orwell the "conscience" of his generation is just and fair praise. In his actions and his writing he is representative. In spite of his frequent wrong-headedness we recognize in him a passionate concern. All of us may not be able to accept all his moral solutions; but we are bound to respect his moral *stance*. For exiles of Orwell's kind a moral stance rather than a moral programme is probably the only way in which they can speak to a fellow-feeling in other men.

It is therefore a temper of heart and mind that we most respond to in Orwell. In trying to define that temper briefly we find ourselves using (and he would have been unlikely to object) old-fashioned phrases. We say, for example, that he stood for *common decency;* and though that phrase is difficult to define and often woolly, with Orwell it defined a hope which he tried to embody in action, it indicated his active commitment to the notion of brotherhood and kindly dealing.

It is easy, too easy, to say that the conditions described in the first part of *Wigan Pier* have almost wholly gone today, and so to feel more comfortable in not taking the book more seriously. One might speculate on what Orwell's own reactions would be if he were to come back to Britain thirty years after *Wigan Pier* was written and fifteen years after his own death. He would certainly have been one of the warmest to welcome all the clear improvements—beginning with the lines of miners' cars which now stand at the pitheads (but on which we too often congratulate ourselves). He would no doubt have enjoyed himself in mordantly attacking those who so much resent the new prosperity that they accuse the working-classes, now that they have TV sets and washing machines, of becoming materialistic. He would certainly have pointed out that for all our increased prosperity plenty of people—many more than most of us wish to recognize—are still living in miserable conditions on little money. He would have seen, what many of us do not wish to see, that there are still two Britains divided at the Trent, that the Saturday afternoon shopping crowds in Bradford and Leicester still *look* different. He would no doubt have pointed out that when he reported in the middle thirties Wigan had over 2,000 houses standing which had been condemned; and that in the sixties, it has been estimated, it would cost 45 million pounds to complete the slum clearance of Oldham alone.

It would have been particularly instructive to hear him comment on whether the increasing attempt now being made to unify the working-classes and the middle-classes as bland consumers seemed near that kind of union between the classes which he urges in the last pages of this book. At that point he would probably have gone, more directly than he was always tempted to do in his writing in the thirties, into what is at bottom his overriding theme —not so much the physical conditions of people but the quality of life offered to them. And on this George Orwell, today, would have been a fascinating and, I think, a disturbing voice.

# Observation and Imagination in Orwell

## by Raymond Williams

Orwell's writing in the 1930s can be conventionally divided between the "documentary" and "factual" work on one hand, and the "fictional" and "imaginative" work on the other. The surface distinction is evident enough: on one hand *Down and Out in Paris and London, The Road to Wigan Pier, Homage to Catalonia,* and such sketches as "The Spike," "A Hanging," "Shooting an Elephant"; on the other hand the four novels *Burmese Days, A Clergyman's Daughter, Keep the Aspidistra Flying,* and *Coming Up for Air.* Yet nothing is clearer, as we look into the work as a whole, than that this conventional division is secondary. The key problem, in all this work, is the relation between "fact" and "fiction": an uncertain relation that is part of the whole crisis of "being a writer."

Literature used not to be divided in these external ways. The rigid distinction between "documentary" and "imaginative" writing is a product of the nineteenth century, and most widely distributed in our own time. Its basis is a naïve definition of the "real world," and then a naïve separation of it from the observation and imagination of men. If there is real life and its recording, on one hand, and a separable imaginative world on the other, two kinds of literature can be confidently distinguished, and this is much more than a formal effect. In naturalist and positivist theories, this effective dualism of "the world" and "the mind" is at least clearly recognizable. But the conventional dualism of most orthodox literary theory has scarcely been noted, let alone challenged. Terms like

"Observation and Imagination in Orwell." From *Orwell*, by Raymond Williams (London: Fontana Books; New York: The Viking Press, 1971). Reprinted by permission of the publishers.

"fiction" and "nonfiction," "documentary" and "imaginative," continue to obscure many of the actual problems of writing.

The unity of Orwell's "documentary" and "imaginative" writing is the very first thing to notice. There were many problems of method, but at least Orwell got past the conventional division, if only in practice. And he saw the division as it actually presented itself to him as something more than a formal problem. He correctly saw it as a problem of social relationships.

> English fiction on its higher levels is for the most part written by literary gents about literary gents for literary gents; on its lower levels it is generally the most putrid "escape" stuff—old maids' fantasies about Ian Hay male virgins, or little fat men's visions of themselves as Chicago gangsters. Books about ordinary people behaving in an ordinary manner are extremely rare, because they can only be written by someone who is capable of standing both inside and outside the ordinary man, as Joyce for instance stands inside and outside Bloom; but this involves admitting that you yourself *are* an ordinary person for nine-tenths of the time, which is exactly what no intellectual ever wants to do.[1]

There is still some unnoticed class feeling in this. Orwell is still seeing from far enough outside to suppose that there are people —a class of people—who are "ordinary" ten-tenths of the time. But to have got as far as he did is something.

> I think the interest of Bloom is that he is an ordinary uncultivated man described from within by someone who can also stand outside him and see him from another angle. Not that Bloom is an absolutely typical man in the street. . . .
> The man in the street is usually described in fiction either by writers who are themselves intellectually men in the street, tho' they may have great gifts as novelists (e.g. Trollope), or by cultivated men who describe him *from outside* (e.g. Samuel Butler, Aldous Huxley).[2]

Cultivated men who describe the man in the street from outside. It is in and through this social deformity, inflicted on him by his class and education, that Orwell reaches for the idea of an extended

1 *Collected Essays*, . . . , I, 230.
2 *Ibid.*, pp. 126, 128.

or even common humanity. His writing in the 1930s is an exploration, in experience and in books, toward such a humanity.

The problem of social relationship is, then, a problem of form. *Down and Out in Paris and London* is in effect a journal. What is put in is the experience of being without money in a modern city: the experience of dishwashers and tramps, of filthy rooms, dosshouses, casual wards. The author is present, but only insofar as these things are happening to him along with others. His own character and motivations are sketched as briefly as those of anyone else met in the kitchen or on the road. He is neither "inside" nor "outside"; he is simply drifting *with* others—exceptionally close to them but within the fact that they are drifting, that this is *happening* to their bodies and minds.

But then compare *A Clergyman's Daughter*. It is a novel about a repressed girl who has a breakdown, goes vagrant, and eventually returns, via teaching, to where she started. Anyone who reads Orwell's other writing of the time will find most of the experiences of the novel elsewhere in other forms. The "Church Times" and the glue-and-brown-paper theatrical armor, and even the "moribund hag who stinks of mothballs and gin, and has to be more or less carried to and from the altar" are to be found in Chapter One of the novel and in Orwell's letters about himself.[3] Again, the girl going vagrant, the hop-picking, Ginger and Deafie, sleeping rough in Trafalgar Square: they are to be found in Chapter Two and the beginning of Chapter Three, and also in Orwell's diary, "Hop-Picking."[4] The point is not the external relation between the writer's "material" and his "process of creation." The interest is almost entirely in the method of handling the author's own presence: the intermediary character of the girl—"inside" when she is caught in the routines of church and teaching; "outside," even amnesiac, when she is drifting on the road. The attempted characterization of the girl as more than a surrogate presence is at times serious and detailed, at times merely functional. But a *sustained* identity, through diversity and dislocation of experiences, cannot yet be realized. And it is interesting that at one point—the night

3 *Ibid.*, pp. 101–102, 103, 105.
4 *Ibid.*, pp. 52–71.

scene in Trafalgar Square, in the first section of Chapter Three—
Orwell makes a conscious literary experiment of a different, impersonal kind, which is very evidently derived from the night-town
chapter in *Ulysses*—the novel that had been so much in his mind
as an example. He remained pleased with this experiment, though
coming to reject his book as a whole.

Orwell's affinity to Joyce—or attempted affinity—is not in our
usual reading. The modern writers Orwell mentions most often, in
his earlier period are Wells, Bennett, Conrad, Hardy, Kipling. In
1940 he makes a different list—Joyce, Eliot, and Lawrence. This
change of emphasis through the 1930s is quite normal and representative. Among earlier writers on his 1940 list, he names Shakespeare, Swift, Fielding, Dickens, Reade, Butler, Zola, and Flaubert.
The critical interest in Shakespeare, Swift, and Dickens can be seen
from his essays. But in the development of his own writing there
are two opposite emphases: the detailed interest in *Ulysses* (notably
in a letter to Brenda Salkeld) at just the time of working on *A
Clergyman's Daughter*, and also, as he said in 1940, "I believe the
modern writer who has influenced me most is Somerset Maugham,
whom I admire immensely for his power of telling a story straightforwardly and without frills." [5]

The names as such do not greatly matter. Literary influence is a
secondary business. What is important is the standpoint, which is
the key to any critical judgment of Orwell. It is easy to say that
*Down and Out in Paris and London* is better than *A Clergyman's
Daughter*, but this ought not to be reduced to the plausible gen-
eralization that he is a better "observer" than "novelist." The real
problem lies deeper, in the available conceptions of "the novel."

"Telling a story straightforwardly and without frills." "Story,"
after all, is the whole question. Maugham is the characteristic Edwardian "storyteller": that is to say, the collector and retailer of
human episodes. Orwell had the material for this (it is usually collected at a distance and in other lands), but only his first novel,
*Burmese Days*, is at all of its kind. Even there, while the plot concerns personal intrigue among an isolated European group on an

[5] *Ibid.*, I, 125–29; II, 24.

Eastern station, the stress is on the complicated social consequences
of imperialism and within this there is what we can now recognize
as the deep Orwell pattern; the man who tries to break from the
standards of his group but who is drawn back into it and, in this
case, destroyed. What is unique about the novel in Orwell's work
is that he creates an entire social and physical milieu within which
the social criticism and the personal break are defined elements.
In all his later novels, the essential form is shaped by what became
separated elements: the personal break, and social criticism through
it, in the novels of the 1930s; the social criticism, with the personal
break inside it, in *Nineteen Eighty-Four.*

That seems a clear development, but it omits the material of
"observation." Having found one form for this, in the journal of
*Down and Out in Paris and London,* Orwell clearly wanted to
incorporate it in a novel. This is the developmental significance of
*A Clergyman's Daughter,* where the direct observation and the fiction are unusually close. But from then on he seems to have accepted the division between "documentary" and "fiction." A possible reshaping of the novel was evaded, or proved too difficult: not,
I would say, because he was "not really a novelist" but because a
problem of consciousness, which he shared with other writers of his
time, emerged as a problem of form.

For Orwell the interest of Joyce had been his direct realization
of "ordinary" experience. It is Bloom he selects from *Ulysses*: that
recording "inside" and "outside" the ordinary man. But this description conceals the problem of the relationship of the novelist to
his character, which is always a form of relationship of the writer
to his world. And the relationship that matters here can be alternatively described as "acceptance" or "passivity." It is an impersonal
form, the logical consequence of James's emphasis on the artist's
"handling" of "matter." It is "the artist refined out of existence,"
observing, recording. Except that in practice it is impossible to observe anything without being in some relationship to it. The apparent relationship, that which is recommended and publicized, is
the "aesthetic"; the "handling" of the matter, the preoccupation
with words, that is Joyce's actual development. But the "matter" can
only be handled in this way—can only be abstracted, stay still to be

"written"—if a particular relationship is in fact assumed. "Acceptance" or "passivity": the difference between the positive and negative descriptions is less important than the fact of the relationship itself—a refraining from intervention, or, more, a seeing no need to intervene, since the availability of the "matter" is the artist's primary and only concern.

Orwell's artistic failure in his novels of the 1930s is in a way, and paradoxically, due to his social achievement. He had known passivity, at least, very closely, as he describes in *Down and Out in Paris and London*. But he had known it not in his capacity as a writer but as a victim. We have seen him describe as an "invasion" the growth of that social consciousness that required his intervention, that made either acceptance or passivity impossible (though he went back to the idea of acceptance and passivity in "Inside the Whale," at a time when the social intervention could be held to have failed).

Then, in shaping a literary form, he created the figure of the intermediary (the "shock-absorber of the bourgeoisie," as he had referred to people like himself) who goes around and to whom things happen. This figure is not Orwell, though it has Orwell's experiences, in *A Clergyman's Daughter* and then in a different way in *Keep the Aspidistra Flying*. The figure is passive; things happen *to* Dorothy, or *to* Comstock. And this pattern releases one element of Orwell's experience—the things that had "happened" to him—but not (or only partly) why they had happened, not the intervening or "invading" consciousness. Dorothy, certainly, is the more passive figure. Comstock, in *Keep the Aspidistra Flying*, is given some of Orwell's whole consciousness: he not only tries to live without money but declares war on money and its system. Comstock is an active and critical figure in all the initial exploration, but increasingly there is a contradiction within the mode of observation. The active and resourceful persistence of Orwell, the impressive survival and remaking of an active self, is steadily cut out, as the accepting observation continues. What begins as a protest becomes a whine, and the reabsorption of Comstock into a world of manipulable objects is accomplished with a kind of perverse triumph; the "character" of the intermediary (like the "char-

acter" of Flory or of Dorothy) becomes the "justification" of the
eventual submission or defeat.

This is the strange transmutation of "acceptance," or "passivity."
In Orwell, because of his uncertainties, it is neither an artistic
discipline nor an acceptable world-view. His final attempt at a
Bloom figure is Bowling in *Coming Up for Air,* written at a recol-
lecting and abstracting distance and perhaps for that reason more
consistent internally. Bowling breaks from an orthodox routine,
like the others, though not into exposure, where things happen to
him, but instead into the past, an old England and his childhood;
and then the experience is of loss, disillusion, disenchantment.
*Coming Up for Air* came after Orwell's crucial political experience
in Spain and its consequences, which we shall have to look at in
detail. But elements of the literary decision are continuous: observation through a limited intermediary, with the limit being the
basis for a deeper pattern: a self-proving of both the need and the
impossibility of a sustained break, with active intervention dwin-
dling to a temporary protest or self-assertion. The significance of
this pattern in the altered world of *Nineteen Eighty-Four* will need
further analysis, when the other changes have been taken into account.

Having failed to solve his profoundly difficult problem in the
novel, Orwell turned to other forms that were in practice more
available. His social and political writing was a direct release of
consciousness, the practical consequence of intervention. "Shooting
an Elephant," for example, is more successful than anything in
*Burmese Days* not because it is "documentary" rather than fiction
—the fiction, as we have seen, similarly relied on things that had
happened to him—but because instead of a Flory an Orwell is
present: a successfully created character in every real sense. Instead
of diluting his consciousness through an intermediary, as the mode
of fiction had seemed to require, he now writes directly and powerfully about his whole experience. The prose is at once strengthened,
as the alternation between an anxious impersonation and a pas-
sively impersonal observation gives way to a direct voice in which
there is more literary creation than in all the more conventionally
"imaginative" attempts. "Shooting an Elephant" is not a docu-

ment; it is a literary work. The distinction between "fiction" and
"nonfiction" is not a matter of whether the experience happened
to the writer, not a distinction between "real" and "imaginary."
The distinction is one of range and consciousness. Written human
experience of an unspecialized and primary kind must always be
recognized as literature. Particular forms, and the origins of the
material, are secondary questions. Orwell began to write literature,
in the full sense, when he found this nonfictional form capable of
realizing his experience directly.

Realizing *his* experience—not only what had happened to him
and what he had observed, but what he felt about it and what he
thought about it, the self-definition of "Orwell," the man inside
and outside the experience. Perhaps the best example is *The Road
to Wigan Pier.* As it happens Orwell's diary notes for this book
have been published.[6] A comparison of the diary and the book is
interesting, for a number of reasons. It is easy enough to find in
the notes the sources of many of the descriptions: of the Brookers'
lodging house, for example, in the opening chapter. But what is
also evident, comparing the two, is the literary process. There is
the expected and necessary development of a scene in the published
version, a fuller and more fluent description, details recollected
from memory. But there is also a saturation of the scene with feeling. Orwell is present and responding, indeed directing response,
as he is only there toward the end in the diary notes. He seems also
to have shifted the lodgers around a bit: Joe, at the Brookers', is
described in the notes as a lodger at a previous house—a house that
is not in the book. So in the book the Brookers' house is not only
given the emphasis of first place but treated as a first, representative
experience ("it struck me that this place must be fairly normal as
lodging-houses in the industrial areas go") when in the diary there
is a preceding and rather different experience.

This is just one small example to illustrate the point about
"documentary" experience. The writer shapes and organizes what
happened to produce a particular effect, based on experience but
then created out of it. The overall organization of *The Road to*

6 *Ibid.,* I, 170–214.

*Wigan Pier* is a major example. In the first part, the "observation"
of the industrial North, one of the key points, in literary terms,
is that Orwell is the isolated observer going around and seeing for
himself. This created character is then used to important effect in
the second half, the argument about socialism, where he is contrasted with the jargon-ridden bourgeois socialists: "The first thing
that must strike any outside observer is that Socialism in its developed form is a theory confined entirely to the middle class." [7]

The external political point is not what is most important here:
"in its developed form" is an infinitely saving clause. The key point
is the persona, the "outside observer"—that is, Orwell. An essential
link between the two parts is indeed this character: "inside" and
then "outside" the experience.

We learn from the diary notes that after some days of wandering
on his own through the Midlands, Orwell was given some political
contacts in Lancashire and met working-class socialists and members of the Unemployed Workers' Movement. Through one of these
contacts he got the chance to go down a mine; and through the
collectors he obtained facts about housing conditions. It is important that he omits most of this experience—an actual social and
political network—in *The Road to Wigan Pier*. Even in the diary,
some of the difficulties are apparent. A local trade-union official
and his wife, "both . . . working-class people," are seen as living
(in a twelve- or fourteen-shilling-a-week estate house) in an "entirely
middle-class" atmosphere. Orwell has his own definition of what
the working class is like. That is, presumably, why he could say,
after meeting these people (who had embarrassed him by calling
him "comrade") and "an electrician who takes a prominent part
in the Socialist movement," that "socialism" was a middle-class
affair. If a workingman is a socialist he is already, presumably,
middle class, the character of the working class being already
known.

But here the political point *is* the literary point. What is created
in the book is an isolated independent observer and the objects of
his observation. Intermediate characters and experiences that do not

7 *The Road to Wigan Pier*, p. 173.

form part of this world—this structure of feeling—are simply omitted. What is left in is "documentary" enough, but the process of selection and organization is a literary act: the character of the observer is as real and yet created as the real and yet created world he so powerfully describes.

All of Orwell's writing until 1937 is, then, a series of works and experiments around a common problem. Instead of dividing them into "fiction" and "documentaries" we should see them as sketches toward the creation of his most successful character, "Orwell." This would not be so successful if it had not been so intensely and painfully lived. The exposure to poverty and suffering and filth and waste was as real as it was deliberate, and the record of the exposure is a remarkable enlargement of our literature. But in and through the exposure a character is being created, who is real in the precise sense that he becomes this writer, this shaping presence. Flory and Dorothy and Comstock, or the later Bowling, are aspects of this character but without his centrality. The only literary form that can contain the full character at this stage is the "non-fiction journal" of an isolated writer exposed to a suffering but unconnecting world. The need to intervene, to force active connections, is the road away from Wigan Pier, back to an indifferent and sleepy and uncaring world, which has to be told about the isolation and the suffering.

At just this point, between the diary and the book, the Spanish war broke out. The writing, and the character, moved into a different dimension.

# George Orwell and the Politics of Truth

## by Lionel Trilling

George Orwell's *Homage to Catalonia* is one of the important documents of our time. It is a very modest book—it seems to say the least that can be said on a subject of great magnitude. But in saying the least it says the most. Its manifest subject is a period of the Spanish Civil War, in which, for some months, until he was almost mortally wounded, its author fought as a soldier in the trenches. Everyone knows that the Spanish war was a decisive event of our epoch, everyone said so when it was being fought, and everyone was right. But the Spanish war lies a decade and a half behind us, and nowadays our sense of history is being destroyed by the nature of our history—our memory is short and it grows shorter under the rapidity of the assault of events. What once occupied all our minds and filled the musty meeting halls with the awareness of heroism and destiny has now become chiefly a matter for the historical scholar. George Orwell's book would make only a limited claim upon our attention if it were nothing more than a record of personal experiences in the Spanish war. But it is much more than this. It is a testimony to the nature of modern political life. It is also a demonstration on the part of its author of one of the right ways of confronting that life. Its importance is therefore of the present moment and for years to come.

A politics which is presumed to be available to everyone is a relatively new thing in the world. We do not yet know very much about it. Nor have most of us been especially eager to learn. In a politics presumed to be available to everyone, ideas and ideals play a great part. And those of us who set store by ideas and ideals have never been quite able to learn that, just because they do have power nowadays, there is a direct connection between their power and another kind of power, the old, unabashed, cynical power of force. We are always being surprised by this. The extent to which Communism made use of unregenerate force was perfectly clear years ago, but many of us found it impossible to acknowledge this fact because Communism spoke boldly to our love of ideas and ideals. We tried as hard as we could to believe that politics might be an idyl, only to discover that what we took to be a political pastoral was really a grim military campaign or a murderous betrayal of political allies, or that what we insisted on calling agrarianism was in actuality a new imperialism. And in the personal life what was undertaken by many good people as a moral commitment of the most disinterested kind turned out to be an engagement to an ultimate immorality. The evidence of this is to be found in a whole literary genre with which we have become familiar in the last decade, the personal confession of involvement and then of disillusionment with Communism.

Orwell's book, in one of its most significant aspects, is about disillusionment with Communism, but it is not a confession. I say this because it is one of the important positive things to say about *Homage to Catalonia,* but my saying it does not imply that I share the *a priori* antagonistic feelings of many people toward those books which, on the basis of experience, expose and denounce the Communist party. About such books people of liberal inclination often make uneasy and rather vindictive jokes. The jokes seem to me unfair and in bad taste. There is nothing shameful in the nature of these books. There is a good chance that the commitment to Communism was made in the first place for generous reasons, and it is certain that the revulsion was brought about by more than sufficient causes. And clearly there is nothing wrong in wishing to record the painful experience and to draw conclusions from it. Nevertheless, human nature being what it is—and in the uneasy readers of such books as well as in the unhappy writers of them— it is a fact that public confession does often appear in an unfortunate light, that its moral tone is less simple and true than we might wish it to be. But the moral tone of Orwell's book is uniquely simple and true. Orwell's ascertaining of certain political facts was not the occasion for a change of heart, or for a crisis of the soul. What he learned from his experiences in Spain of course pained him very much, and it led him to change his course of conduct. But it did not destroy him; it did not, as people say, cut the ground from under him. It did not shatter his faith in what he had previously believed, nor weaken his political impulse, nor even change its direction. It produced not a moment of guilt or self-recrimination.

Perhaps this should not seem so very remarkable. Yet who can doubt that it constitutes in our time a genuine moral triumph? It suggests that Orwell was an unusual kind of man, that he had a temper of mind and heart which is now rare, although we still respond to it when we see it.

It happened by a curious chance that on the day I agreed to write this essay as the introduction to the new edition of *Homage to Catalonia,* and indeed at the very moment that I was reaching for the telephone to tell the publisher that I would write it, a young man, a graduate student of mine, came in to see me, the purpose of his visit being to ask what I thought about his doing an essay on George Orwell. My answer, naturally, was ready, and when I had given it and we had been amused and pleased by the coincidence, he settled down for a chat about our common subject. But I asked him not to talk about Orwell. I didn't want to dissipate in talk what ideas I had, and also I didn't want my ideas crossed with his, which were sure to be very good. So for a while we merely exchanged bibliographical information, asking each other which of Orwell's books we had read and which we owned. But then, as if he could not resist making at least one remark about Orwell himself, he said suddenly in a very simple and matter-of-fact way, "He was a virtuous man." And we sat there, agreeing at length about this statement, finding pleasure in talking about it.

It was an odd statement for a young man to make nowadays, and I suppose that what we found so interesting about it was just this oddity—its point was in its being an old-fashioned thing to say. It was archaic in its bold commitment of sentiment, and it used an archaic word with an archaic simplicity. Our pleasure was not merely literary, not just a response to the remark's being so appropriate to Orwell, in whom there was indeed a quality of an earlier and simpler day. We were glad to be able to say it about anybody. One doesn't have the opportunity very often. Not that there are not many men who are good, but there are few men who, in addition to being good, have the simplicity and sturdiness and activity which allow us to say of them that they are virtuous men, for somehow to say that a man "is good," or even to speak of a man who "is virtuous," is not the same thing as saying, "He is a virtuous man." By some quirk of the spirit of the language, the form of that sentence brings out the primitive meaning of the word virtuous, which is not merely moral goodness, but also fortitude and strength in goodness.

Orwell, by reason of the quality that permits us to say of him that he was a virtuous man, is a figure in our lives. He was not a genius, and this is one of the remakable things about him. His not being a genius is an element of the quality that makes him what I am calling a figure.

It has been some time since we in America have had literary figures—that is, men who live their visions as well as write them, who *are* what they write, whom we think of as standing for something as men because of what they have written in their books. They preside, as it were, over certain ideas and attitudes. Mark Twain was in this sense a figure for us, and so was William James. So too were Thoreau, and Whitman, and Henry Adams, and Henry James, although posthumously and rather uncertainly. But when in our more recent literature the writer is anything but anonymous, he is likely to be ambiguous and unsatisfactory as a figure, like Sherwood Anderson, or Mencken, or Wolfe, or Dreiser. There is something about the American character that does not take to the idea of the figure as the English character does. In this regard, the English are closer to the French than to us. Whatever the legend to the contrary, the English character is more strongly marked than ours, less reserved, less ironic, more open in its expression of willfulness and eccentricity and cantankerousness. Its manners are cruder and bolder. It is a demonstrative character—it shows itself, even shows off. Santayana, when he visited England, quite gave up the common notion that Dickens' characters are caricatures. One can still meet an English snob so thunderingly shameless in his worship of the aristocracy, so explicit and demonstrative in his adoration, that a careful, modest, ironic American snob would be quite bewildered by him. And in modern English literature there have been many writers whose lives were demonstrations of the principles which shaped their writing. They lead us to be aware of the moral personalities that stand behind the work. The two Lawrences, different as they were, were alike in this: that they assumed the roles of their belief and acted them out on the stage of the world. In different ways this was true of Yeats, and of Shaw, and even of Wells. It is true of T. S. Eliot, for all that he has spoken against the claims of personality in literature. Even E. M. Forster, who makes so much of privacy, acts out in public the role of the private man, becoming for us the very spirit of the private life. He is not merely a writer, he is a figure.

Orwell takes his place with these men as a figure. In one degree or another they are geniuses, and he is not; if we ask what it is he stands for, what he is the figure of, the answer is: the virtue of not being a genius, of fronting the world with nothing more than one's simple, direct, undeceived intelligence, and a respect for the powers one does have, and the work one undertakes to do. We admire geniuses, we love them, but they discourage us. They are great concentrations of intellect and emotion, we feel that they have soaked up all the available power, monopolizing it and leaving none for us. We feel that if we cannot be as they, we can be nothing. Beside them we are so plain, so hopelessly threadbare. How they glitter, and with what an imperious way they seem to deal with circumstances, even when they are wrong! Lacking their patents of nobility, we might as well quit. This is what democracy has done to us, alas—told us that genius is available to anyone, that the grace of ultimate prestige may be had by anyone, that we may all be princes and potentates, or saints and visionaries and holy martyrs, of the heart and mind. And then when it turns out that we are no such thing, it permits us to think that we aren't much of anything at all. In contrast with this cozening trick of democracy, how pleasant seems the old, reactionary Anglican phrase that used to drive people of democratic leanings quite wild with rage—"my station and its duties."

Orwell would very likely have loathed that phrase, but in a way he exemplifies its meaning. And it is a great relief, a fine sight, to see him doing this. His novels are good, quite good, some better than others, some of them surprising us by being so very much better than their modesty leads us to suppose they can be, all of them worth reading; but they are clearly not the work of a great or even of a "born" novelist. In my opinion, his satire on Stalinism, *Animal Farm*, was overrated—I think people were carried away by someone's reviving systematic satire for serious political purposes. His critical essays are almost always very fine, but sometimes they do not fully meet the demands of their subject—as, for example, the essay on Dickens. And even when they are at their best, they seem to have become what they are chiefly by reason of the very plainness of Orwell's mind, his simple ability to look at things in a downright, undeceived way. He seems to be serving not some dashing daimon but the plain, solid Gods of the Copybook Maxims. He is not a genius—what a relief! What an encouragement. For he communicates to us the sense that what he has done any one of us could do.

Or could do if we but made up our mind to do it, if we but surrendered a little of the cant that comforts us, if for a few weeks we paid no attention to the little group with which we habitually exchange opinions, if we took our chance of being wrong or inadequate, if we looked at things simply and directly, having in mind only our intention of finding out what they really are, not the prestige of our great intellectual act of looking at them. He liberates us. He tells us that we can understand our political and social life merely by looking around us; he frees us from the need for the inside dope. He implies that our job is not to be intellectual, certainly not to be intellectual in this fashion or that, but merely to be intelligent according to our lights—he restores the old sense of the democracy of the mind, releasing us from the belief that the mind can work only in a technical, professional way and that it

must work competitively. He has the effect of making us believe
that we may become full members of the society of thinking men.
That is why he is a figure for us.

In speaking thus of Orwell, I do not mean to imply that his birth
was presided over only by the Gods of the Copybook Maxims and
not at all by the good fairies, or that he had no daimon. The good
fairies gave him very fine free gifts indeed. And he had a strong
daimon, but it was of an old-fashioned kind and it constrained him
to the paradox—for such it is in our time—of taking seriously the
Gods of the Copybook Maxims and putting his gifts at their service. Orwell responded to truths of more than one kind, to the bitter, erudite truths of the modern time as well as to the older and
simpler truths. He would have quite understood what Karl Jaspers
means when he recommends the "decision to renounce the absolute
claims of the European humanistic spirit, to think of it as a stage
of development rather than the living content of faith." But he
was not interested in this development. What concerned him was
survival, which he connected with the old simple ideas that are
often not ideas at all but beliefs, preferences, and prejudices. In the
modern world these had for him the charm and audacity of newly
discovered truths. Involved as so many of us are, at least in our
literary lives, in a bitter metaphysics of human nature, it shocks
and dismays us when Orwell speaks in praise of such things as responsibility, and orderliness in the personal life, and fair play, and
physical courage—even of snobbery and hypocrisy because they
sometimes help to shore up the crumbling ramparts of the moral
life.

It is hard to find personalities in the contemporary world who
are analogous to Orwell. We have to look for men who have considerable intellectual power but who are not happy in the institu-
tionalized life of intellectuality; who have a feeling for an older
and simpler time, and a guiding awareness of the ordinary life of
the people, yet without any touch of the sentimental malice of
populism; and a strong feeling for the commonplace; and a direct,
unabashed sense of the nation, even a conscious love of it. This
brings Péguy to mind, and also Chesterton, and I think that Orwell
does have an affinity with these men—he was probably unaware of

it—which tells us something about him. But Péguy has been dead for quite forty years, and Chesterton (it is a pity) is at the moment rather dim for us, even for those of us who are Catholics. And of course Orwell's affinity with these men is limited by their Catholicism, for although Orwell admired some of the effects and attitudes of religion, he seems to have had no religious tendency in his nature, or none that went beyond what used to be called natural piety.

In some ways he seems more the contemporary of William Cobbett and William Hazlitt than of any man of our own century. Orwell's radicalism, like Cobbett's, refers to the past and to the soil. This is not uncommon nowadays in the social theory of literary men, but in Orwell's attitude there is none of the implied aspiration to aristocracy which so often marks literary agrarian ideas; his feeling for the land and the past simply served to give his radicalism a conservative—a conserving—cast, which is in itself attractive, and to protect his politics from the ravages of ideology. Like Cobbett, he does not dream of a new kind of man, he is content with the old kind, and what moves him is the desire that this old kind of man should have freedom, bacon, and proper work. He had the passion for the literal actuality of life as it is really lived which makes Cobbett's *Rural Rides* a classic, although a forgotten one; his own *The Road to Wigan Pier* and *Down and Out in Paris and London* are in its direct line. And it is not the least interesting detail in the similarity of the two men that both had a love affair with the English language. Cobbett, the self-educated agricultural laborer and sergeant major, was said by one of his enemies to handle the language better than anyone of his time, and he wrote a first-rate handbook of grammar and rhetoric; Orwell was obsessed by the deterioration of the English language in the hands of the journalists and pundits, and nothing in *Nineteen Eighty-Four* is more memorable than his creation of Newspeak.

Orwell's affinity with Hazlitt is, I suspect, of a more intimate temperamental kind, although I cannot go beyond the suspicion, for I know much less about Orwell as a person than about Hazlitt. But there is an unquestionable similarity in their intellectual temper which leads them to handle their political and literary opinions

in much the same way. Hazlitt remained a Jacobin all his life, but
his unshakable opinions never kept him from giving credit when
it was deserved by a writer of the opposite persuasion, not merely
out of chivalrous generosity but out of respect for the truth. He
was the kind of passionate democrat who could question whether
democracy could possibly produce great poetry, and his essays in
praise of Scott and Coleridge, with whom he was in intense political disagreement, prepare us for Orwell on Yeats and Kipling.

The old-fashionedness of Orwell's temperament can be partly
explained by the nature of his relation to his class. This was by
no means simple. He came from that part of the middle class whose
sense of its status is disproportionate to its income, his father having been a subordinate officer in the Civil Service of India, where
Orwell was born. (The family name was Blair, and Orwell was
christened Eric Hugh; he changed his name, for rather complicated
reasons, when he began to write.) As a scholarship boy he attended
the expensive preparatory school of which Cyril Connolly has given
an account in *Enemies of Promise*. Orwell appears there as a school
"rebel" and "intellectual." He was later to write of the absolute
misery of the poor boy at a snobbish school. He went to Eton on
a scholarship, and from Eton to Burma, where he served in the
police. He has spoken with singular honesty of the ambiguousness
of his attitude in the imperialist situation. He disliked authority
and the manner of its use, and he sympathized with the Burmese;
yet as the same time he saw the need for authority and he used it,
and he was often exasperated by the natives. When he returned to
England on leave after five years of service, he could not bring himself to go back to Burma. It was at this time that, half voluntarily,
he sank to the lower depths of poverty. This adventure in extreme
privation was partly forced upon him, but partly it was undertaken
to expiate the social guilt which he felt he had incurred in Burma.
The experience seems to have done what was required of it. A
year as a casual worker and vagrant had the effect of discharging
Orwell's guilt, leaving him with an attitude toward the working
class that was entirely affectionate and perfectly without sentimentality.

His experience of being declassed, and the effect which it had upon him, go far toward defining the intellectual quality of Orwell and the particular work he was to do. In the thirties the middle-class intellectuals made it a moral fashion to avow their guilt toward the lower classes and to repudiate their own class tradition. So far as this was nothing more than a moral fashion, it was a moral anomaly. And although no one can read history without being made aware of what were the grounds of this attitude, yet the personal claim to a historical guilt yields but an ambiguous principle of personal behavior, a still more ambiguous basis of thought. Orwell broke with much of what the English upper middle class was and admired. But his clear, uncanting mind saw that, although the morality of history might come to harsh conclusions about the middle class and although the practicality of history might say that its day was over, there yet remained the considerable residue of its genuine virtues. The love of personal privacy, of order, of manners, the ideal of fairness and responsibility—these are very simple virtues indeed and they scarcely constitute perfection of either the personal or the social life. Yet they still might serve to judge the present and to control the future.

Orwell could even admire the virtues of the lower middle class, which an intelligentsia always finds it easiest to despise. His remarkable novel, *Keep the Aspidistra Flying,* is a *summa* of all the criticisms of a commercial civilization that have ever been made, and it is a detailed demonstration of the bitter and virtually hopeless plight of the lower-middle-class man. Yet it insists that to live even in this plight is not without its stubborn joy. Péguy spoke of "fathers of families, those heroes of modern life"—Orwell's novel celebrates this biological-social heroism by leading its mediocre, middle-aging poet from the depths of splenetic negation to the acknowledgment of the happiness of fatherhood, thence to an awareness of the pleasures of marriage, and of an existence which, while it does not gratify his ideal conception of himself, is nevertheless his own. There is a dim, elegiac echo of Defoe and of the early days of the middle-class ascendancy as Orwell's sad young man learns to cherish the small personal gear of life, his own bed and chairs and saucepans—his own aspidistra, the ugly, stubborn, organic emblem of survival.

We may say that it was on his affirmation of the middle-class virtues that Orwell based his criticism of the liberal intelligentsia. The characteristic error of the middle-class intellectual of modern times is his tendency to abstractness and absoluteness, his reluctance to connect idea with fact, especially with personal fact. I cannot recall that Orwell ever related his criticism of the intelligentsia to the implications of *Keep the Aspidistra Flying,* but he might have done so, for the prototypical act of the modern intellectual is his abstracting himself from the life of the family. It is an act that has something about it of ritual thaumaturgy—at the beginning of our intellectual careers we are like nothing so much as those young members of Indian tribes who have had a vision or a dream which gives them power on condition that they withdraw from the ordinary life of the tribe. By intellectuality we are freed from the thralldom to the familial commonplace, from the materiality and concreteness by which it exists, the hardness of the cash and the hardness of getting it, the inelegance and intractability of family things. It gives us power over intangibles and imponderables, such as Beauty and Justice, and it permits us to escape the cosmic ridicule which in our youth we suppose is inevitably directed at those who take seriously the small concerns of the material quotidian world, which we know to be inadequate and doomed by the very fact that it is so absurdly *conditioned*—by things, habits, local and temporary customs, and the foolish errors and solemn absurdities of the men of the past.

The gist of Orwell's criticism of the liberal intelligentsia was that they refused to understand the conditioned nature of life. He never quite puts it in this way but this is what he means. He himself knew what war and revolution were really like, what government and administration were really like. From first-hand experience he knew what communism was. He could truly imagine what nazism was. At a time when most intellectuals still thought of politics as a nightmare abstraction, pointing to the fearfulness of the nightmare as evidence of their sense of reality, Orwell was using the imagination of a man whose hands and eyes and whole body were part of his thinking apparatus. Shaw had insisted upon remaining sublimely unaware of the Russian actuality; Wells had pooh-

poohed the threat of Hitler and had written off as anachronisms the very forces that were at the moment shaping the world—racial pride, leader-worship, religious belief, patriotism, love of war. These men had trained the political intelligence of the intelligentsia, who now, in their love of abstractions, in their wish to repudiate the anachronisms of their own emotions, could not conceive of directing upon Russia anything like the same stringency of criticism they used upon their own nation. Orwell observed of them that their zeal for internationalism had led them to constitute Russia their new fatherland. And he had the simple courage to point out that the pacifists preached their doctrine under condition of the protection of the British navy, and that, against Germany and Russia, Gandhi's passive resistance would have been of no avail.

He never abated his anger against the established order. But a paradox of history had made the old British order one of the still beneficent things in the world, and it licensed the possibility of a social hope that was being frustrated and betrayed almost everywhere else. And so Orwell clung with a kind of wry, grim pride to the old ways of the last class that had ruled the old order. He must sometimes have wondered how it came about that he should be praising sportsmanship and gentlemanliness and dutifulness and physical courage. He seems to have thought, and very likely he was right, that they might come in handy as revolutionary virtues—he remarks of Rubashov, the central character of Arthur Koestler's novel *Darkness at Noon,* that he was firmer in loyalty to the revolution than certain of his comrades because he had, and they had not, a bourgeois past. Certainly the virtues he praised were those of survival, and they had fallen into disrepute in a disordered world.

Sometimes in his quarrel with the intelligentsia Orwell seems to sound like a leader-writer for the *Times* in a routine wartime attack on the highbrows.

> . . . The general weakening of imperialism, and to some extent of the whole British morale, that took place during the nineteen thirties, was partly the work of the left-wing intelligentsia, itself a kind of growth that sprouted from the stagnation of the Empire.

74 Lionel Trilling

> The mentality of the English left-wing intelligentsia can be studied in half a dozen weekly and monthly papers. The immediately striking thing about all these papers is their generally negative querulous attitude, their complete lack at all times of any constructive suggestion. There is little in them except the irresponsible carping of people who have never been and never expect to be in a position of power.

> During the past twenty years the negative faineant outlook which has been fashionable among the English left-wingers, the sniggering of the intellectuals at patriotism and physical courage, the persistent effort to chip away at English morale and spread a hedonistic, what-do-I-get-out-of-it attitude to life, has done nothing but harm.

But he was not a leader-writer for the *Times*. He had fought in Spain and nearly died there, and on Spanish affairs his position had been the truly revolutionary one. The passages I have quoted are from his pamphlet, *The Lion and the Unicorn,* a persuasive statement of the case for socialism in Britain.

Toward the end of his life Orwell discovered another reason for his admiration of the old middle-class virtues and his criticism of the intelligentsia. Walter Bagehot used to speak of the political advantages of *stupidity,* meaning by the word a concern for one's own private material interests as a political motive which was preferable to an intellectual, theoretical interest. Orwell, it may be said, came to respect the old bourgeois virtues because they were stupid—that is, because they resisted the power of abstract ideas. And he came to love things, material possessions, for the same reason. He did not in the least become what is called "anti-intellectual" —this was simply not within the range of possibility for him—but he began to fear that the commitment to abstract ideas could be far more maleficent than the commitment to the gross materiality of property had ever been. The very stupidity of things has something human about it, something meliorative, something even liberating. Together with the stupidity of the old unthinking virtues it stands against the ultimate and absolute power which the unconditioned idea can develop. The essential point of *Nineteen Eighty-Four* is just this, the danger of the ultimate and absolute power which mind can develop when it frees itself from conditions, from the bondage of things and history.

But this, as I say, is a late aspect of Orwell's criticism of intellectuality. Through the greater part of his literary career his criticism was simpler and less extreme. It was as simple as this: that the contemporary intellectual class did not think and did not really love the truth.

In 1937 Orwell went to Spain to observe the civil war and to write about it. He stayed to take part in it, joining the militia as a private. At that time each of the parties still had its own militia units, although these were in process of being absorbed into the People's Army. Because his letters of introduction were from people of a certain political group in England, the ILP,[1] which had connections with the POUM,[2] Orwell joined a unit of that party in Barcelona. He was not at the time sympathetic to the views of his comrades and their leaders. During the days of interparty strife, the POUM was represented in Spain and abroad as being a Trotskyist party. In point of fact it was not, although it did join with the small Trotskyist party to oppose certain of the policies of the dominant Communist party. Orwell's own preference, at the time of his enlistment, was for the Communist party line, and because of this he looked forward to an eventual transfer to a Communist unit.

It was natural, I think, for Orwell to have been a partisan of the Communist program for the war. It recommended itself to most people on inspection by its apparent simple common sense. It proposed to fight the war without any reference to any particular political idea beyond a defense of democracy from a fascist enemy. When the war was won, the political and social problems would be solved, but until the war should be won, any debate over these problems was to be avoided as leading only to the weakening of the united front against Franco.

Eventually Orwell came to understand that this was not the practical policy he had at first thought it to be. His reasons need not be reiterated here—he gives them with characteristic cogency and

[1] Independent Labor Party.
[2] *Partido Obrero de Unificación Marxista*—Party of Marxist Unification.

modesty in the course of his book, and under the gloomy but probably correct awareness that, the economic and social condition of
Spain being what it was, even the best policies must issue in some
form of dictatorship. In sum, he believed that the war was revolutionary or nothing, and that the people of Spain would not fight
and die for a democracy which was admittedly to be a bourgeois
democracy.

But Orwell's disaffection from the Communist party was not the
result of a difference of opinion over whether the revolution should
be instituted during the war or after it. It was the result of his discovery that the Communist party's real intention was to prevent the
revolution from ever being instituted at all—"The thing for which
the Communists were working was not to postpone the Spanish
revolution till a more suitable time, but to make sure it never happened." The movement of events, led by the Communists, who had
the prestige and the supplies of Russia, was always to the right, and
all protest was quieted by the threat that the war would be lost if
the ranks were broken, which in effect meant that Russian supplies
would be withheld if the Communist lead was not followed. Meanwhile the war was being lost because the government more and more
distrusted the non-Communist militia units, particularly those of
the Anarchists. "I have described," Orwell writes, "how we were
armed, or not armed, on the Aragon front. There is very little doubt
that arms were deliberately withheld lest too many of them should
get into the hands of the Anarchists, who would afterwards use
them for a revolutionary purpose; consequently, the big Aragon
offensive which would have made Franco draw back from Bilbao
and possibly from Madrid, never happened."

At the end of April, after three months on the Aragon front,
Orwell was sent to Barcelona on furlough. He observed the change
in morale that had taken place since the days of his enlistment—
Barcelona was no longer the revolutionary city it had been. The
heroic days were over. The militia, which had done such splendid
service at the beginning of the war, was now being denigrated in
favor of the People's Army, and its members were being snubbed as
seeming rather queer in their revolutionary ardor, not to say danger-

ous. The tone of the black market and of privilege had replaced the old idealistic puritanism of even three months earlier. Orwell observed this but drew no conclusions from it. He wanted to go to the front at Madrid, and in order to do so he would have to be transferred to the International Column, which was under the control of the Communists. He had no objection to serving in a Communist command and, indeed, had resolved to make the transfer. But he was tired and in poor health and he waited to conclude the matter until another week of his leave should be up. While he delayed, the fighting broke out in Barcelona.

In New York and in London the intelligentsia had no slightest doubt of what had happened—could not, indeed, have conceived that anything might have happened other than what they had been led to believe had actually happened. The Anarchists, together with the "Trotskyist" POUM—so it was said—had been secreting great stores of arms with a view to an uprising that would force upon the government their premature desire for collectivization. And on the third of May their plans were realized when they came out into the streets and captured the Telephone Exchange, thus breaking the united front in an extreme manner and endangering the progress of the war. But Orwell in Barcelona saw nothing like this. He was under the orders of the POUM, but he was not committed to its line, and certainly not to the Anarchist line, and he was sufficiently sympathetic to the Communists to wish to join one of their units. What he saw he saw as objectively as a man might ever see anything. And what he records is now, I believe, accepted as the essential truth by everyone whose judgment is worth regarding. There were no great stores of arms cached by the Anarchists and the POUM—there was an actual shortage of arms in their ranks. But the Communist-controlled government had been building up the strength of the Civil Guard, a gendarmerie which was called "nonpolitical" and from which workers were excluded. That there had indeed been mounting tension between the government and the dissident forces is beyond question, but the actual fighting was touched off by acts of provocation committed by the government itself—shows of military strength, the call to all private persons to give up arms, attacks

on Anarchist centers, and, as a climax, the attempt to take over the
Telephone Exchange, which since the beginning of the war had
been run by the Anarchists.

It would have been very difficult to learn anything of this in New
York or London. The periodicals that guided the thought of left-
liberal intellectuals knew nothing of it, and had no wish to learn.
As for the aftermath of the unhappy uprising, they appeared to
have no knowledge of that at all. When Barcelona was again quiet
—some six thousand Assault Guards were imported to quell the
disturbance—Orwell returned to his old front. There he was severely
wounded, shot through the neck; the bullet just missed the wind-
pipe. After his grim hospitalization, of which he writes so lightly,
he was invalided to Barcelona. He returned to find the city in process of being purged. The POUM and the Anarchists had been
suppressed; the power of the workers had been broken and the
police hunt was on. The jails were already full and daily becoming
fuller—the most devoted fighters for Spanish freedom, men who
had given up everything for the cause, were being imprisoned under the most dreadful conditions, often held incommunicado, often
never to be heard of again. Orwell himself was suspect and in danger because he had belonged to a POUM regiment, and he stayed
in hiding until, with the help of the British consul, he was able to
escape to France. But if one searches the liberal periodicals, which
have made the cause of civil liberties their own, one can find no
mention of this terror. Those members of the intellectual class who
prided themselves upon their political commitment were committed
not to the fact but to the abstraction.[3]

[3] In looking through the files of *The Nation* and the *New Republic* for the
period of the Barcelona fighting, I have come upon only one serious contradiction of the interpretation of events that constituted the editorial position of both
periodicals. This was a long letter contributed by Bertram Wolfe to the correspon-
dence columns of *The Nation*. When this essay first appeared, some of my friends
took me to task for seeming to imply that there were no liberal or radical intellectuals who did not accept the interpretations of *The Nation* and the *New Republic*. There were indeed such liberal or radical intellectuals. But they were
relatively few in number and they were treated with great suspiciousness and
even hostility by the liberal and radical intellectuals as a class. It is as a class
that Orwell speaks of the intellectuals of the left in the thirties, and I follow him
in this.

And to the abstraction they remained committed for a long time to come. Many are still committed to it, or nostalgically wish they could be. If only life were not so tangible, so concrete, so made up of facts that are at variance with each other; if only the things that people say are good things were really good; if only the things that are pretty good were entirely good and we were not put to the ever-lasting necessity of qualifying and discriminating; if only politics were not a matter of power—*then* we should be happy to put our minds to politics, *then* we should consent to think!

But Orwell had never believed that the political life could be an intellectual idyl. He immediately put his mind to the politics he had experienced. He told the truth, and told it in an exemplary way, quietly, simply, with due warning to the reader that it was only one man's truth. He used no political jargon, and he made no recriminations. He made no effort to show that his heart was in the right place, or the left place. He was not interested in where his heart might be thought to be, since he knew where it was. He was interested only in telling the truth. Not very much attention was paid to his truth—*Homage to Catalonia* sold poorly in England, it had to be remaindered, it was not published in America, and the people to whom it should have said most responded to it not at all.

Its particular truth refers to events now far in the past, as in these days we reckon our past. It does not matter the less for that—this particular truth implies a general truth which, as now we cannot fail to understand, must matter for a long time to come. And what matters most of all is our sense of the man who tells the truth.

# Inside *Which* Whale?

## *by E. P. Thompson*

There are no good causes left, not because of any lack of causes, but because within Natopolitan culture the very notion of a good cause is a source of embarrassment. "The passive attitude will come back," Orwell predicted in *Inside the Whale* (which was published in 1940—the same year in which Auden revised *Spain*):

> The passive attitude will come back, and it will be more consciously passive than before. Progress and reaction have both turned out to be swindles. Seemingly there is nothing left but quietism—robbing reality of its terrors by simply submitting to it. Get inside the whale —or rather, admit that you are inside the whale (for you *are*, of course). Give yourself over to the world-process, stop fighting against it or pretending that you control it; simply accept it, endure it, record it.

But, as Orwell reminded, the yearning for the Jonah myth is not heroic; "the whale's belly is simply a womb big enough for an adult": "Short of being dead, it is the final, unsurpassable stage of irresponsibility."

And yet *Inside the Whale* must itself be read as an apology for quietism. It is true that the attitude which Orwell commended in Henry Miller—"fiddling with his face towards the flames"—may be seen as a gesture of personal dissociation from the "world-process," even as an act of protest. But the fiddling of Henry Miller is close to the exchange of ironic points of light between the Just. And in this essay we can observe the way in which Orwell's mind, exposed to the same European disasters as was Auden's,

"Inside *Which* Whale?" From *Out of Apathy*, by E. P. Thompson (London: New Left Books, Stevens & Sons Ltd). Reprinted by permission of Sweet & Maxwell Ltd.

entered into a similar pattern of default. Orwell's profound political pessimism tended in the same direction as Auden's spiritual
pessimism, and once again, at a certain point the problem was
simply given up.

We do not mean that this pessimism was without adequate *cause.*
*Homage to Catalonia* gives a part of the background; the collapse
of the Popular Front gives the rest. 1940 was a nadir of hope which
may be compared with 1948–51. We must give credit to the stubborn criticism, the assertion of the values of intellectual integrity,
which Orwell also voiced throughout the 1936–46 decade. But since
the *form* of Orwell's pessimism has contributed a good deal to
Natopolitan ideology, it is necessary to examine the premises. The
presumption of a determined pattern of institutional change for
the worse turns out, at bottom, to be uncommonly like the assumption of original sin. The premise is found in the phrase—"Progress
and reaction have both turned out to be swindles"—so reminiscent
of Auden's dismissal of a "low, dishonest decade." "Swindle" is an
imprecise tool of analysis, a noise of disgust. Orwell had first used
the notion that "progress is a swindle" in *The Road to Wigan Pier,*
in the context of his polemic against the euphoric scientific Uto-
pianism of Wells; now the notion is attached to "progress" at large,
and, in particular, to all manifestations of Communism. Throughout *Inside the Whale* the same tone of wholesale, indiscriminate
rejection can be heard whenever Communist ideas or organization
come under discussion:

> The years 1935–39 were the period of anti-Fascism and the Popular
> Front, the heyday of the Left Book Club, when red duchesses and
> "broad-minded" deans toured the battlefields of the Spanish war and
> Winston Churchill was the blue-eyed boy of the *Daily Worker.*

Yes? True, there *was* one duchess and one dean, and the *Daily
Worker* on occasion found Churchill a useful stick to beat Cham-
berlain with. But was this *all* that anti-Fascism, the Popular Front,
and the Left Book Club movement added up to? Of course, Orwell
himself did not think so, although the reader could scarcely guess
from this that *The Road to Wigan Pier* was one of the most successful and widely discussed of Left Books.

What was, in 1940, a provocation, is accepted by many, in 1960, as a sober historical evaluation. Indeed, one wonders what on earth the post-war generation can make of the "history" presented, out of context and out of chronological sequence, in the Penguin *Selected Essays*; it must appear like an endless football game in which one side (Fascism, Reaction) is invisible, while the other side (Anti-Fascism, Communism, Progress) spend their whole time fouling each other or driving the ball into their own goal. Orwell is like a man who is raw all down one side and numb on the other. He is sensitive—sometimes obsessionally so—to the least insincerity upon his left, but the inhumanity of the right rarely provoked him to a paragraph of polemic. To the right ("decent people," "average thinking person"), every allowance; to the left ("bearded fruit-juice drinkers who come flocking towards the smell of 'progress' like bluebottles to a dead cat"), no quarter. What is noticeable about Orwell's characterization of Communism in *Inside the Whale* is that time after time his prejudices are angry, antagonistic responses to the ruling left orthodoxy, so laying the basis for a new orthodoxy-by-opposition. He assumes Communism to be a Bad Thing, driven forward by the mainspring of its own bad will—the powerdrives of the Russian State and the deracinated romanticism of Western intellectuals. A sentence such as this:

> The Communist movement in Western Europe began as a movement for the violent overthrow of capitalism, and degenerated within a few years into an instrument of Russian foreign policy.

contains a half-truth which, at a certain level of policy and of ideology, is an aid to the interpretation of the evolution of the Third International. But at another level none of the historical questions are asked. How far was this "degeneration" caused by (or accelerated by?) the European counter-revolution which culminated in Fascism? How far was it fostered by the active anti-Soviet policies of Nazi Germany, Conservative Britain? How far, within this context, did the Communist argument—that the "heartland" of Socialism must be defended—have validity? How far did the foreign policy of Litvinov *deserve* to command the support of Western socialists, as against that of Ribbentrop, Laval or Sir

Samuel Hoare? How far, anyway, is it a statement about the *de-formities* of the movement, but not about the nature and function of the movement itself?

But to all such questions the tone of disgust ("swindle") was sufficient reply. In consequence, the complex and contradictory character of the Communist movement, the inner tensions, were never seen. Who would suppose, from Orwell's indiscriminate re-jection, that there were many Communists from Tom Wintringham to Ralph Fox who shared his criticisms of orthodoxy? That all Communist intellectuals were not public school boys with a "taste for violence," that they were not all "squashily pacifist" and "the kind of person who is always somewhere else when the trigger is pulled"? That, within the rigid organization and orthodoxy, the Communist movement in the thirties (and forties) retained (in differing degrees in different contexts) a profoundly democratic content, in the innumerable voluntary initiatives and the deep sense of political responsibility of the rank and file? But Orwell was blind to all such discriminations; and in this he anticipated the wholesale rejection of Communism which became a central feature of Natopolitan ideology. And this failure was important, not only because it helped to blind a later generation to the forces within Communism making for its transformation, but because it denied the possibility of *hope* within the pattern of social change wherever Communist influence could be detected. This denial of *hope* had the force of an irrational taboo; and, as Orwell himself noted, "even a single taboo can have an all-round crippling effect upon the mind" (*The Prevention of Literature*). In this case the taboo contaminated all confidence in social man and imprisoned Orwell in the negations of *1984*.

We should also note another characteristic device of Orwell's polemic. He continually replaced the examination of objective situations by the imputation of motive. If it is assumed that Com-munism was a Bad Thing, then the problem is to discover the mo-tivations which made intellectuals turn towards it. Intellectuals in the thirties (Orwell discovered) were in revolt because of the "soft-ness and security of life in England" of the "soft-boiled emancipated middle class" (notice the anti-intellectual tone of *soft-boiled,* and that *emancipated* has become a sneer-word). Internationalism was really the patriotism of the deracinated, the appeal to collective security was really "warmongering," and the Left was Reaction. Ironically, Orwell was providing arguments which later became prominent in Natopolitan double-think.

It is true that specious apologetics and romantic attitudes were to be found amongst the Left intelligentsia in the thirties. Orwell succeeds in pinpointing those which most irritated him. What he does *not* do is suggest that any other, more honorable, motivations might have coexisted with the trivia. And in this he falsifies the record. Nor does he tell us anything of the actual choices with which the intellectuals of his generation were faced within an objective context of European crisis. Popular Front, Left Book Club and the rest are seen, not as a political response within a definite political context, but as the projection of the neuroses and petty motives of a section of the English middle class.

It was in this essay, more than any other, that the aspirations of a generation were buried; [1] not only was a political movement, which embodied much that was honorable, buried, but so also was the notion of disinterested dedication to a political cause. Orwell, by indicting the cause as a swindle *and* by ridiculing the motives of those who supported it, unbent the very "springs of action." He sowed within the disenchanted generation the seeds of a profound self-distrust. Socialist idealism was not only discounted, it was also *explained away,* as the function of middle-class guilt, frustration or ennui.

The final consequence of disenchantment was delayed. Europe itself was beleaguered by the forces of negation. The post-war generation, while indoctrinated thoroughly with the legend of the "swindle" of the thirties, has only a hazy understanding of the forties. Perhaps it is necessary to recall that at one time nearly all Europe was lost to Fascism, and that Jewish people, trade unionists (people), liberal intellectuals (people), and Communists (people) were—well, *suffering*. The war was nearly lost. If it had been lost

---

[1] It was not the only essay (Koestler's *The Yogi and the Commisar* was of equal importance), nor was its effect immediate; but the disenchanted of 1945–49 retired to the positions which Orwell had already prepared.

it would probably have made a difference—even though "all . . . epochs are transient details," we would have had to die in *that* epoch. It was not won by quietism, but by people who still held, in less articulate form, to Auden's "illusion" that they were, willy-nilly, actors in a critical contest in history. Few of those who fought had any "taste for violence." Communists were not somewhere else when the trigger was pulled. People thought that they were *making* the "world-process"—not as they would wish to do, but in an extremity of necessity. And the voices of personal motive tended to get drowned (dangerously so, as subsequent Communist history shows) in the winds of the historical imperative.

It was after the war and after Hiroshima, as the Four Freedoms fell apart and the Cold War commenced, that people turned back to *Inside the Whale.* Once again, disillusion in the power politics of Communism was felt more keenly (and seen more clearly) than in the power politics of the West. Prompted by Orwell and by Koestler, the disenchanted fastened on the problem of motive. All the obstinate questions of actual context— Had they *really* been wrong to regard the Spanish War as a critical prelude to world war? Could Western liberals (and quietists) so *wholly* absolve themselves from responsibility for the post-war evolution of Stalinism?—these could be set on one side. It was assumed that whatever happened necessarily happened in this way; that because the democratic elements in the Communist tradition were submerged by the authoritarian, this was inevitably so, and revealed the "true" character of Communism; and that whatever could be observed in Communist history or practice which could not be assimilated to an essential diabolism must—by definition—have been attached to the movement by accident or deceit. And the disenchanted turned to rend the Stalinist apologist as the author of their betrayal. He had asked for it, it is true, and was sometimes the immediate agent. But the real author was inextricably involved in the context of European revolution and counter-revolution, in the backward Russian villages, in the jails of Horthy, in the desperation of the oppressed and the unemployed. But the disenchanted failed to distinguish between their own perfectionist illusions and the aspirations which had fed them. It was a long job to "unearth the whole offence" by "accurate scholarship." Easier to dismiss the whole episode as a "swindle" and the motives which had led to their involvement as corrupt.

It was easier, also, for the disenchanted intellectual to see himself as the helpless victim of a "world-process." It was hopeless to attempt any rally of the disenchanted—

> For by superior energies; more strict
> Affiance in each other; faith more firm
> In their unhallowed principles, the bad
> Have fairly earned a victory o'er the weak,
> The vacillating, inconsistent good.
>
> Wordsworth, *Excursion*, IV, 304 *et seq.*

Disillusion, reason, self-interest—all seemed to lead to passivity. A "world-process" plus corrupt motives equals original sin. "All societies and epochs are transient details . . ." turns out to be much the same as "progress and reaction" are "swindles." Auden and Orwell had converged at a common point. Whether you are inside a whale or regard all whales as transient details you will not bother much about navigation.

Somewhere around 1948 the *real* whale of Natopolis swam along this way through the seas of the Cold War. After watching the splashings about of the disenchanted, with mean speculation in its small eyes, it opened its jaws and gulped—not, indeed, so that the intellectuals could sit in a distinguished posture in its belly, but in order to add nourishment to its digestive system. The reduction of political idealism to suspect motive was a welcome titbit. By the fifties, literature from Dostoievsky to Conrad had been ransacked for confirmation. Psychologists were called in to testify. Novels, plays and theses were written, displaying not only Communism but also radicalism as projections of the neuroses of maladjusted intellectuals. The theme entered the repertoire of Hollywood spy dramas. The intellectual stood appalled before the seduction of his own more generous impulses. The least chirrup of his undernourished social conscience was silenced lest it should turn out to be a "taste for violence" or a vestige of guilt. "And behind that again" —warned Mr. Kingsley Amis—"lies perhaps your relations with your parents." The Natopolitan intellectual was disabled by self-distrust no less than the Stalinist intellectual was disabled by fear of reverting to bourgeois modes of thought. The very fact of an intellectual espousing any public cause (unless as a career politician) was enough to touch off suspicion. The Western disenchanted delivered themselves over, by their own hand and in confessional mood, to McCarthyism, just as an earlier generation of Communist intellectuals had, by their capitulation before the "infallible" party, delivered themselves over to Zhdanov and to Beria. In Natopolitan culture today, no swearword is more devastating than "romantic," just as the "Utopian" or "idealist" is the butt of Stalinist abuse. It was left to Mr. Amis to make the ultimate definition of political romanticism: "an irrational capacity to become inflamed by interests and causes that are not one's own, that are outside oneself" (*Socialism and the Intellectuals,* 1957).

It was from the lampoons of the disenchanted that the post-war generation picked up bits of "history." The revolt of Oxford intellectuals in the thirties, one young socialist tells us, "(though quite sincere) was safe, like the tantrums of a spoilt child":

> You could yell and scream in the nursery—because you knew the nursery walls were built to last. You could even kick and scratch old Nanny—because you knew she would never desert you and would even forgive you in the end. (David Marquand in the *Manchester Guardian,* August 18, 1958.)

The self-emasculated had perhaps received the shabby epitaph which they deserved. They had passed on to the next generation only the great negative of impotence.

But it is not the epitaph which the historical thirties deserved, any more than the self-flagellation of Wordsworth's Solitary is a true comment upon the men of the Corresponding Societies. It may be years before an objective judgment upon the period can be made. It will not be made until speculations upon motive are placed firmly back into the whole context of the time. Men were not placed in some pure climate of choice, but in a context of savage counter-revolution and military politics which none had chosen. If their choices had been wiser, world war might conceivably have been

averted or limited. If their actions had been more self-centered, then
the war would certainly have been lost. And it is difficult to see how
the evidence of the thirties and forties (taken together) can be read
as an irrevocable verdict upon the darkness of the human heart.
The worst evil was defeated. And if every form of evil—power-lust,
sadism and the corrosion of humanism into abstractions of power—
were displayed on the side of the victor, so also was self-sacrifice,
heroism and every generous quality in superabundance. The annals
of Communism alone contain enough martyrs to furnish a cycle
of religions. More than a sound of mockery should come down to
us from Jarama Ridge and the concentration camps. In our recoil
from the oppressors we forget the integrity of the oppressed. If
good, wise and great went to the wall—some to face the firing
squads of their own side—we forget that this death was also an
affirmation:

> Mock mockers after that
> That would not lift a hand maybe
> To help good, wise or great
> To bar that foul storm out, for we
> Traffic in mockery.

# George Orwell as a Writer of Polemic

## by John Wain

It is impossible to criticize an author's work adequately until you have understood what kind of books he was writing; there was a time, in fact, when the art of criticism pivoted largely on the doctrine of the "kinds." A Renaissance critic saw literature as divided (by Nature, not by human interference) into "kinds," and his idea of the function of criticism was to determine, in case of doubt, what "kind" a work belonged to, and how it measured up to the standards of that kind. Thus, a work could be censured for having excellences which were not proper to its kind, as well as for not having the ones that were. If Orwell's work has been grotesquely misjudged, and I think it has, the explanation is simple: it lies in the complete withering-away of the notion of literary kinds—so complete that we have abandoned the very word, and now speak of *genres,* as the Duchess told Alice to speak in French if she couldn't think of the English for a thing.

The "kind" to which Orwell's work belongs is the polemic. All of it, in whatever form—novels, essays, descriptive sketches, volumes of autobiography—has the same object: to implant in the reader's mind a point of view, often about some definite, limited topic (the Spanish Civil War, the treatment of tramps in casual wards, the element of reactionary propaganda in boys' fiction) but in any case about an issue over which he felt it was wrong not to take sides. A writer of polemic is always a man who, having himself chosen what side to take, uses his work as an instrument for strengthening the support for that side. English literature is full of polemic writing;

"George Orwell as a Writer of Polemic." From *Essays on Literature and Ideas,* by John Wain (London: Macmillan & Company, Ltd.). Reprinted by permission of Macmillan & Company, Ltd., Curtis Brown Ltd., and St. Martin's Press, Inc.

some of it is direct exhortation, but mostly it belongs, nominally,
to some other kind such as fiction or poetry, and is often in danger
of being under-rated by the standards of that kind. G. K. Chesterton's novels, for instance, are, considered simply as novels, beneath
criticism; but as polemic they do add up to something—one has the
impression of a clever and high-spirited man who really believes in
his religion, and where they fail is where this impression ceases to
come over, or comes over falsely, rather than where they cease to
be good as novels. I believe that nine-tenths of the bad criticism
one reads is traceable to the neglect of this simple and ancient doctrine. And with that I leave the topic of Orwell's stature as a man
of letters. It can safely wait; indeed, by comparison with the urgent
task of exposing and clarifying his basic ideas, it can safely be neg-
lected altogether. It is by his ideas, rather than by any particular
skill in putting them over, that he will live. And if that is an over-
simplification, it is one that Orwell himself would have agreed to.
"All art is propaganda," he said once; a half-truth, as we see if we
ask "What is *Hamlet* propaganda for?" But the fact that Orwell
read other people's books as polemic is a pointer to how we should
read him.

If we consider Orwell as a writer of polemic, then, it will at least
help to guide us past the initial paradox—the fact that his work,
with so many and such crippling faults, contrives to be so valuable
and interesting. He was a novelist who never wrote a satisfactory
novel, a literary critic who never bothered to learn his trade properly, a social historian whose history was full of gaps. Yet he matters. For *as polemic* his work is never anything less than magnificent; and the virtues which the polemic kind demands—urgency,
incisiveness, clarity and humor—he possessed in exactly the right
combination.

This method might also preserve us from the error that has beset
the most recent commentators on Orwell: namely, a tendency to
refer everything back to his personal character. A man has a right
to have his opinions criticized at the level of opinion, no matter
how many embarrassing anecdotes we can remember about him.
Not that there is any point in denying that Orwell's opinions were,
to some extent, the almost automatic result of his upbringing and

environment. Everyone's are. His hatred of sham and cant, for instance, was obviously due at least partly to the fact of his springing from the underside of the *haute bourgeoisie*—what he called "the lower-upper-middle-class." These were the people who tended to cling to the myth of an ascendancy that, in hard practical terms, they had long since forfeited; consequently their lives were a network of evasions and petty half-deceptions. As he put it:

> You lived, so to speak, at two levels simultaneously. Theoretically you knew all about servants and how to tip them, although in practice you had one, or at most two, resident servants. Theoretically you knew how to wear your clothes and how to order a good dinner, although in practice you could never afford to go to a decent tailor or a decent restaurant. Theoretically you knew how to shoot and ride, although in practice you had no horses to ride and not an inch of ground to shoot over. (*The Road to Wigan Pier,* Chapter VIII.)

Most Englishmen of Orwell's generation who were brought up in that particular tradition rejected it pretty decisively, sooner or later; his renunciation was unusually spectacular, because his impatience with any kind of falsity was unusually urgent. His real name was Eric Blair, but after the very beginning of his career he rejected both Christian name and surname, though for different reasons; "Eric" because it was redolent of public-school stories and would, he felt, identify its owner with the wrong kind of English tradition, the tradition of Talbot Baines Reed if not actually that of Dean Farrar; "Blair" because it was a Scotch name, and he was irked by the mass confidence trick which the Scots had played on the English in getting themselves automatically deferred to as more industrious, honest, brave, capable.

But, while granting all this, we must be careful. There are some of Orwell's beliefs that are almost invariably dismissed as products of his personal situation, mere reflexes, hardly to be dignified with the term "ideas" at all—and it is easy to make this dismissal too readily. His wish to identify himself with the working class is an example. Some of the quainter sides of his character certainly came out over this business; when the spirit moved him, and it often moved him, he would launch into a grotesque imitation of a working man in such details as pouring his tea into his saucer to cool

it. He has very frankly told us, in the autobiographical passages of
*The Road to Wigan Pier,* how a good deal of this feeling was traceable to the events of his life. Five years in the Indian Imperial Police had given him a hatred of oppression which amounted to a
mania, and, when he returned in 1927 to an England in which the
working class was already menaced by unemployment, he naturally
transferred to them the feelings he had been having about the
Burmese. "I had reduced everything to the simple theory that the
oppressed are always right and the oppressors are always wrong: a
mistaken theory, but the natural result of being one of the oppressors yourself. I felt that I had got to escape not merely from imperialism but from every form of man's dominion over man."
Hence the emotional identification with the manual worker, which,
as we know, he occasionally carried to comic lengths. As when, for
instance, he begins an illustrative anecdote by saying, "On the day
when King George V's body passed through London on its way
to Westminster, I happened to be caught for an hour or two in
the crowd in Trafalgar Square." It wouldn't do, you see, to admit
that he had gone along out of a natural curiosity to see the funereal
pomp. Yet it must have been a formidable crowd in which a physically active man could be "caught," against his will, for "an hour
or two"! This kind of thing raises an indulgent smile. But—and
this is where we must go carefully—it does not follow that we can
dismiss Orwell's ideas about the working class as a mere idiosyn-
crasy, belonging to the sphere of biography rather than that of
ideas. "If there is hope," thinks the desperate man trapped in the
hell of 1984, "it lies in the proles." As usual, we turn to the non-
fiction for a clear exposition of the theme, and we find it in the
essay, *Looking Back on the Spanish War.*

> The intelligentsia are the people who squeal loudest against Fas-
> cism, and yet a respectable proportion of them collapse into defeat-
> ism when the pinch comes. They are far-sighted enough to see the
> odds against them, and moreover they can be bribed—for it is evi-
> dent that the Nazis think it worthwhile to bribe intellectuals. With
> the working class it is the other way about. Too ignorant to see
> through the trick that is being played on them, they easily swallow
> the promises of Fascism, yet sooner or later they always take up the

struggle again. They must do so, because in their own bodies they always discover that the promises of Fascism cannot be fulfilled. To win over the working class permanently, the Fascists would have to raise the general standard of living, which they are unable and probably unwilling to do. The struggle of the working class is like the growth of a plant. The plant is blind and stupid, but it knows enough to keep pushing upwards towards the light, and it will do this in the face of endless discouragements.

Substitute the more generalized "totalitarian" for "Fascist" in that passage, and you have the fundamental reason for Orwell's wish to line up with the working man. Not that his attitude is sentimental or optimistic. The working man is like a plant, and the plant is "blind and stupid." But that blindness and stupidity represent a last-ditch defense of human freedom. It is a characteristically Orwellian position: grim, realistic, even bleak. But at least it enables us to dispose of the charge that his attitude to "the proles" was a piece of literary man's *naïveté*. And that should encourage us to make the attempt, unfashionable though it is, to consider his ideas as ideas, his arguments as arguments, rather than tag along in the fashionable search for "personal" explanations that will safely put his books in the freak-show along with his shooting-stick and his home-made cigarettes.

Of course Orwell was in no sense an abstruse thinker. His political ideas were of the simplest. They were, in character, undisguisedly ethical; he believed in the necessity of being frank and honest, and he believed in freedom for everyone, with no authoritarian rule and no tyrannizing, economic or otherwise. These were the twin pillars on which all his ideas rested, and, while it may be convenient to take them one at a time for the purposes of rough-and-ready analysis, it is not possible to separate them for long. In his eyes they were one and the same. With the direct clear-sightedness that was his greatest intellectual gift, he saw that modern tyranny works *by means of* dishonesty and evasion. And not only "modern"; Charles II, the last English king who still cherished hopes of a strong-arm repressive rule over his people, is on record as having believed that government was "a safer and easier thing where the authority was believed infallible and the faith and submission of the people were implicit." *Homo sapiens* naturally wishes to be free to do as he likes, not enslaved, not caged. Very well, the dictators answer, we will destroy the appetite for freedom; no one will fight for something he is not aware of lacking. Hence the Ministry of Truth, hence Doublethink, Newspeak, and the other devices for preventing people from grasping what is happening to them. It is a curious fact that Orwell's picture of the future is not particularly terrifying from the material point of view. Although he lived to see the atom bomb, lived to see it dropped twice on defenceless people, his vision of 1984 does not include extinction weapons. Airstrip One is permanently at war, in a vague sort of way, and every now and then a guided missile comes over and kills a few people in the street, but it is a guided missile of the type familiar in 1944, the type that were exploding round him as he wrote the book. He is not interested in extinction weapons because, fundamentally, they do not frighten him as much as spiritual ones; the death of his body is a misfortune for a man, but it is not as bad as the death of his spirit; Orwell approved of Gandhi's opinion that "there must be a limit to what we will do in order to stay alive," even if he laughed at him for fixing that limit "well on this side of chicken broth." Besides, a tyrant who has people shot is a tyrant easy to recognize. Killing people is not likely to remain unnoticed, for their absence will sooner or later be remarked on; but killing their instinct for freedom, degrading their status as human beings, can remain unnoticed almost indefinitely. If this view is incorrect, it took the Hungarians to prove it—and Orwell can't be blamed for not foreseeing *that*. So he made it his business to point at the very heart of the situation—the power of a totalitarian state to erase the past, by tampering with the records, until any trace of dissent becomes as if it had never been. This is an important point, so he must be allowed to speak for himself; it is worth the tedium of a rather long quotation:

> In the past people deliberately lied, or they unconsciously coloured what they wrote, or they struggled after the truth, well knowing that they must make many mistakes; but in each case they believed that "the facts" existed and were more or less discoverable. And in practice there was always a considerable body of fact which would have

been agreed to by almost everyone. If you look up the history of the last war in, for instance, the *Encyclopaedia Britannica*, you will find that a respectable amount of the material is drawn from German sources. A British and a German historian would disagree deeply on many things, even on fundamentals, but there would still be that body of, as it were, neutral fact on which neither would seriously challenge the other. It is just this common basis of agreement, with its implication that human beings are all of one species of animal, that totalitarianism destroys. Nazi theory indeed specifically denies that such a thing as "the truth" exists. There is, for instance, no such thing as "Science." There is only "German Science," "Jewish Science," etc. The implied objective of this line of thought is a nightmare world in which the Leader, or some ruling clique, controls not only the future but *the past*. If the Leader says of such and such an event, "It never happened"—well, it never happened. If he says that two and two are five—well, two and two are five. This prospect frightens me much more than bombs—and after our experiences of the last few years that is not a frivolous statement. (*Looking Back on the Spanish War*)

That, then, was the prospect that frightened him more than bombs, which accounts for the relative absence of bombs from his nightmare of the future. High explosive was unpopular already. He felt the need to indicate the more deadly danger, and to follow this up by pointing out how easily any of us might unconsciously help to increase that danger. Anyone who talked or wrote in vague, woolly language, for instance—language which tended to veil the issues it claimed to be discussing—he denounced as an enemy. The language of free men must, he held, be vivid, candid, *truthful*. Those who took refuge in vagueness did so because they had something to hide. Once more we must quote at some length.

In our time, political speech and writing are largely the defence of the indefensible. Things like the continuance of British rule in India, the Russian purges and deportations, the dropping of the atom bombs on Japan, can indeed be defended, but only by arguments which are too brutal for most people to face, and which do not square with the professed aims of political parties. Thus political language has to consist largely of euphemism, question-begging and sheer cloudy vagueness. Defenceless villages are bombarded from the air, the inhabitants driven out into the countryside, the cattle machine-gunned, the huts set on fire with incendiary bullets: this is called *pacification*. Millions of peasants are robbed of their farms and sent trudging along the roads with no more than they can carry: this is called *transfer of population* or *rectification of frontiers*. People are imprisoned for years without trial, or shot in the back of the neck or sent to die of scurvy in Arctic lumber camps: this is called *elimination of unreliable elements*. Such phraseology is needed if one wants to name things without calling up mental pictures of them. . . . The inflated style is itself a kind of euphemism. A mass of Latin words falls upon the facts like soft snow, blurring the outlines and covering up all the details. The great enemy of clear language is insincerity. When there is a gap between one's real and one's declared aims, one turns as it were instinctively to long words and exhausted idioms, like a cuttlefish squirting out ink (*Politics and the English Language*).

The relationship between style and character, always familiar from the adage *Le style, c'est l'homme même,* seemed to Orwell one of the most important truths; and it all came circling back to his conviction that the price of freedom is candor. Why is Orwell himself a model of English prose style? *Because he was not frightened.* He had a relatively simple subject-matter to express, it is true, and his famous clarity may be admitted to arise partly from that fact; but, after all, the great majority of people who write have no very complex subject-matter, and one rarely finds clarity and forthrightness that would pass the Orwellian test. Saying straight out what you mean, even in a liberal democracy, will always call for a certain moral effort; a little too much anxiety to stand well with exeryone, to be a good fellow all round, and your style is ruined—as we see from any edition of any weekly paper. But Orwell carried the argument one stage further. He noticed that large numbers of modern people, uneasy in a world that seemed to be drifting, had attached themselves to the anchorage of some form of orthodoxy. It might be Roman Catholicism, it might be Communism, it might be anarchism or pacifism. For most practical purposes he lumped them together. Any word ending with "ism" was enough to draw his ridicule. Thus in *The Road to Wigan Pier* we find him saying, bluntly, "The Communist and the Catholic are not saying the same thing, in a sense they are even saying opposite things, and each would gladly boil the other in oil if circumstances permitted; but from the point of view of an outsider they are very much alike." And this opposition was not merely temperamental, not merely a product of his rôle as the "born rebel." It was based on a number of firmly reasoned arguments. One of the chief of these concerned the nature of the imagination. It is of particular interest to those of us who write, but not by any means to them alone, since "where there is no vision the people perish." Let us look at it for a moment.

Orwell believed that an author who sacrificed his intellectual freedom was finished as an author. The ability to create, to imagine story and character, depended, in his view, on the free and wide-ranging use of the mind. And this is exactly what an orthodoxy, of any kind, is designed to prevent. Anyone who accepts a system of beliefs, who declares himself in favor of this or that Ism, lock, stock and barrel, is bound to commit himself to a certain amount of hypocrisy, conscious or otherwise. No intelligent person ever lived who could swallow *all* the details of some overarching dogma such as Marxism or Roman Catholicism. People who embrace these beliefs do so, in the main, for reasons which are not, strictly, intellectual. Many Christians, for example, believe that everything that is best and noblest in the European tradition is rooted in Christianity, that if Christianity goes it will not be long before all values, all sanctions, go too. Consequently they give their support to the Church because they feel that it is more important for the Church to survive than for them to be one hundred per cent clear of intellectual hypocrisy. Equally obviously, many Communists, particularly in the East, embrace their creed because they feel that with all its faults it will be a means of ridding them of the servility of their former way of life; they know, if they have any intelligence, that the intellectual dogmas of dialectical materialism are riddled with absurdities and shortcomings, but they accept the absurdities along with the rest. It is human, understandable and consistent that people should do this. And if they are grocers or gravediggers, there is not much harm done. They can still go about their work efficiently, even though they have accepted a certain amount of built-in censorship. But if they are writers, they are finished. That is Orwell's point, and I have never seen it refuted. The key essay in which he expressed this view is "The Prevention of Literature," reprinted in _Shooting an Elephant_. Here is a snatch:

> The journalist is unfree, and is conscious of unfreedom, when he is forced to write lies or suppress what seems to him important news: the imaginative writer is unfree when he has to falsify his subjective feelings, which from his point of view are facts. He may distort and caricature reality in order to make his meaning clearer, but he cannot misrepresent the scenery of his own mind: he cannot say with any conviction that he likes what he dislikes, or believes what he disbelieves. If he is forced to do so, the only result is that his creative faculties dry up. Nor can he solve the problem by keeping away from controversial topics. There is no such thing as genuinely nonpolitical literature, and least of all in an age like our own, when fears, hatreds, and loyalties of a directly political kind are near to the surface of everyone's consciousness. Even a single taboo can have an all-round crippling effect upon the mind, because there is always the danger that any thought which is freely followed up may lead to the forbidden thought.

This is the sort of thing we should remember when we make use of Orwell as an ally in the cold war. Of course he hated Soviet totalitarianism; of course he wrote a poignant animal-fable to express the tragic plight of the Russian people, caught in its grasp; but that does not mean that every smooth-talking window-dresser of his works, Conservative in politics, Roman Catholic in religion, can claim him as a supporter. Next time you read one of the books or essays put out by these gentlemen, remember Orwell's contemptuous remark about "all the smelly little orthodoxies which are now contending for our souls." In his nostrils, _every_ orthodoxy smelt bad—and he gave his reasons clearly and openly.

That phrase about the orthodoxies comes from Orwell's essay on Dickens, and I should like to turn, next, to his work as a literary critic. Now, obviously this has serious faults. It is, in fact, "amateur" in both the good and the bad senses. He thought of his literary criticism as merely an extension of his everyday activities. Reading is one of the normal activities of anyone interested in the world he is living in; if you read, you will come to prefer some books to others, or alternatively to detest some more than others; it is reasonable, in that case, to write articles about them. An article about a book doesn't differ, significantly, from an article about anything else. That was his attitude. Unfortunately it is true that literary criticism is a trade you have to learn; it *is* specialized, just as the writing of history is specialized; and the reader of Orwell soon learns that he must overlook flaws which are the result of not having thought deeply enough about the nature of criticism. His amateurism permitted him to talk only about what caught his attention, and brush the rest aside; he had the amateur's untroubled assumption that what matters about a work of art is what he thinks about it, rather than what it is. His essay on Tolstoy's criticism of *King Lear*, for instance, is in many ways superb; apart from the fact that it contains a number of acute remarks about both Shakespeare and Tolstoy, it serves as a vehicle for some of Orwell's most moving and impressive utterances about human life. It is worth a dozen tidily accurate essays with no loose ends or ragged edges. But, all the same, it does contain some misstatements, even absurdities, which arise from his characteristic lack of care over literary *nuances*. He says, for instance, that Shakespeare has told the story rather clumsily: "It is too drawnout and has too many characters and sub-plots. . . . Indeed it would probably be a better play if Gloucester and both his sons were eliminated." This innocent remark reveals, first, that he cannot have taken the slightest trouble to read what other critics have said about the play, and secondly that, for all his acuteness, he was incapable of the sort of attentive, close study that we expect of a real literary critic. How odd that he could have read, or seen, *King Lear* without realizing that the thousand and one echoes and interpenetrations between the main plot and the sub-plot are the chief technical means that Shakespeare is using! Any undergraduate, who had done a little reading and been to a lecture or two, could have put him right: but then the undergraduate would have missed all the things Orwell has seen. What he has seen, as usual, is the broad general "message" of the play, and how it meshes in with life: both life in general, and Tolstoy's own peculiar life in particular, hitting off so many features of the great Russian's own situation that in the end he turned and denounced it angrily. It is an essay that will keep its relevance as long as human beings have moral problems; but, as a strictly "literary" essay, it was, in many ways, doomed before it started. Compare it, for instance, with the famous essay on *Boys' Weeklies.* Orwell's treatment of *King Lear* and his treatment of *The Magnet* (a boys' paper that ran for about thirty years) are both brilliant, but they are not different enough. He treats them both as documents, expressing a certain attitude to life; and while it is true that he rather admires the attitude to life he finds in *King Lear,* and doesn't think much of the one he finds in *The Magnet,* this doesn't set them sufficiently far apart. If all the texts of these works were lost, and we had nothing but Orwell's essay to go on, we should never be able to tell, from reading it, that Shakespeare was as far superior to the amiable author of *The Magnet* as, in fact, he is.

So it isn't for "literary criticism," in the real sense, that one reads Orwell's essays on books, any more than one reads his novels as "imaginative work" in the real sense. It is all the same thing; a blunt, honest presentation of the important issues as he saw them, usually with a strong "practical" bias. But it must be said, before we leave his criticism, that in a few instances this limitation actually operates as a strength. The essay on Kipling is perhaps the best example. Kipling is not an author of subtle shades or recondite effects; his work presents no technical problems, even simple ones like that of the relationship of plot and sub-plot in *King Lear;* it was possible for Orwell to arrive at a valid estimate of him merely by being clear-sighted about his subject-matter. The result is the best defense that Kipling has ever had, because it stresses that, while often wrong and stupid, he was never merely silly.

> He identified himself with the ruling power and not with the opposition. In a gifted writer this seems to us strange and even disgusting, but it did have the advantage of giving Kipling a certain grip on reality. The ruling power is always faced with the question, "In such and such circumstances, what would you do?," whereas the opposition is not obliged to take responsibility or make any real decisions. Where it is a permanent and pensioned opposition, as in England, the quality of its thought deteriorates accordingly.

It was characteristic of Orwell that he found at least that much to admire in Kipling. He saw that it didn't excuse Kipling's follies, or make him a more pleasing writer, but in his eyes a readiness to make decisions and *do* something was worth a great deal of subtlety. That remark about the "permanent and pensioned opposition," for instance, touches on a theme he often returned to. It ceased to be true, of course, after the sweeping electoral victory of that opposition in 1945, but during most of Orwell's writing life it was true that the people he felt bound to support, the English Left, were a long way from the centers of power and tended to cultivate a sterile, nagging brand of criticism. With this he had no sympathy at all. All his life, one of his favorite butts was the "progressive" who cares more that his ideas should be "advanced" than that they should be realistic and workable. In his essay on Wells, for instance, he remarked:

> What has kept England on its feet during the past year [1940–41]? In part, no doubt, some vague idea about a better future, but chiefly the atavistic emotion of patriotism, the ingrained feeling of the English-speaking peoples that they are superior to foreigners. For the last twenty years the main object of English left-wing intellectuals has been to break this feeling down, and if they had succeeded, we might be watching the S.S. men patrolling the London streets at this moment.

That is the characteristic tone: what interests him is not the theoretically tidy or impressive solution, but the one that *works*— and works here and now. And this brings us back to the point about his "kind" as a polemic writer. All the strengths and weaknesses of his work come out of this center. For instance, it will seem to some people staggering and even culpable that Orwell should have steadfastly refused to tackle, in his work, the problem that he constantly acknowledged to be the most urgent of all—that of faith. As early as *A Clergyman's Daughter*, there is a remarkable outburst on the futility of human life if it is not sustained by faith. And as late as the essay on Arthur Koestler (1944) we find him saying, "The real problem is how to restore the religious attitude while accepting death as final." If this was "the real problem," some will ask, why didn't he address himself to it? Because—and we will give him his own voice again—"privation and brute labour have to be abolished before the real problems of humanity can be tackled. The major problem of our time is the decay of the belief in personal immortality, and it cannot be dealt with while the average human being is either drudging like an ox or shivering in fear of the secret police" (*Looking Back on the Spanish War*). So Orwell postponed the ultimate task and labored at the one nearest at hand. And when we come to weigh up his achievements, it may be that we shall count this sacrifice as one of them. For, to a writer, it *is* a sacrifice to admit that so many other things matter more urgently than writing. Orwell put the claim of his fellow-man consistently before his own, and the paradox is that it is this spirit, rather than any specifically literary quality, that will keep his work alive.

# Orwell as Satirist

## by Stephen J. Greenblatt

In "Such, Such Were the Joys . . ." Orwell exposed the myth of the English public school; in *Burmese Days* he attacked the myth of the British Raj; in two short journals of the 1930s—*Down and Out in Paris and London* (1933) and *The Road to Wigan Pier* (1937) —he chronicled the breakdown of the myth of capitalism. The latter documents are not technically satires, for they propose merely to record Orwell's own experience during the depression years, and their merits presumably lie in the author's renowned "honesty" and in his clear, concise prose style. But in choosing his details, in ordering his experience, Orwell employed all the devices he later used in *Animal Farm* and *1984*. Orwell's prose is never the simple, colorless "window pane" he claims as his ideal; rather it always involves what Northrop Frye calls "the mythical patterns of experience, the attempts to give form to the shifting ambiguities and complexities of unidealized existence." [1] The satirist takes the vast mass of empirical data and, consciously or unconsciously, selects those details, almost always grotesque and ugly, which justify his attitude toward experience. As Frye observes, "The satirist has to select his absurdities, and the act of selection is a moral act." [2] One might add a creative act as well, for it is in the organizing, arranging, and shaping of his material that the satirist's art is revealed. Satirical prose, then, is not a transparent medium through which the reader is given a view of reality, but a very peculiar lens, which renders distorted and often

"Orwell as Satirist." From *Three Modern Satirists*, by Stephen J. Greenblatt (New Haven: Yale University Press, 1965). Reprinted by permission of Yale University Press Ltd.

1 Northrop Frye, *Anatomy of Criticism* (Princeton, 1957), p. 223.
2 Frye, p. 224.

grotesque images of society. In *Down and Out in Paris and London,*
for example, Orwell's experience in the world of the drunks, beg-
gars, tramps, thieves, and prostitutes who live on the fringes of "civilized" society is seen as a descent into a seething, squalid inferno, a
fantasy world where all is ugliness, noise, decay, rot, collapse: "It
was a very narrow street—a ravine of tall, leprous houses, lurching
towards one another in queer attitudes, as though they had all been
frozen in the act of collapse." [3]

Even when Orwell asserts that his prose is devoid of satiric intent,
his work assumes the forms of ironic fantasy or myth, not of realism.
In the spirit of a scientist observing the behavior of a peculiar species of rodent, Orwell "relates" in *Down and Out* a grotesquely
comical story told by Charlie, "one of the local curiosities." The tale
is vicious and sadistic, permeated with demonic imagery and an atmosphere of horror which the ironic humor only heightens. Charlie,
a debauched youth, cruelly rapes a peasant girl whose parents had
sold her into slavery. In the few moments of violent lust in a cellar
flodded with a garish red glare, "a heavy, stifling red, as though the
light were shining through bowls of blood," Charlie asserts that "I
captured the supreme happiness, the highest and most refined emotion to which human beings can attain . . . That is Love. That
was the happiest day of my life" (pp. 11–12). Orwell is careful to
point out three times that Charlie "was a youth of family and education," and the tale is most clearly a satire exposing the sexual cruelty that lurks beneath middle-class morality. But Orwell denies all
ironic purpose, concluding blandly, "He was a curious specimen,
Charlie. I describe him, just to show what diverse characters could
be found flourishing in the Coq d'Or quarter" (p. 12).

The demonic imagery is even more apparent in Orwell's superb
description of his life as a *plongeur* in the subbasements of a huge
Parisian hotel:

> The kitchen was like nothing I had ever seen or imagined—a stifling,
> low-ceilinged inferno of a cellar, red lit from the fires, and deafening
> with oaths and the clanging of pots and pans . . . The chargings to
> and fro in the narrow passages, the collisions, the yells, the struggling

[3] Orwell, *Down and Out in Paris and London* (New York, Berkeley, 1959), p. 5.

> with crates and trays and blocks of ice, the heat, the darkness, the
> furious festering quarrels which there was no time to fight out—they
> pass description.     [p. 48]

Clearly Orwell is going beyond straight realism and is creating, in
the description of a plongeur's life, as he does later with the miner's
existence in *The Road to Wigan Pier,* an image of a modern hell
and a sweeping condemnation of capitalism. Orwell's brilliant, imaginative descriptions stand, in their great power, as an eloquent
justification of the art of satire, for the heavy didacticism of many of
Orwell's essays is overwhelmed by the force of his mythic descriptions:

> All round was the lunar landscape of slag-heaps, and to the north,
> through the passes, as it were, between the mountains of slag, you
> could see the factory chimneys sending out their plumes of smoke.
> The canal path was a mixture of cinders and frozen mud, criss-
> crossed by the imprints of innumerable clogs, and all round, as far
> as the slag-heaps in the distance, stretched . . . pools of stagnant
> water. . . . It seemed a world from which vegetation had been ban-
> ished; nothing existed except smoke, shale, ice, mud, ashes and foul
> water.     [*Wigan,* p. 96]

The true vehicle, then, for Orwell's bitter condemnation of capitalism is not the pseudo-philosophical essay but the satirical description, the world seen as a grotesque charnel house, stifling hot or horribly cold, reeking with the obscene stench of human sweat and ex-
crement, choked with filth and the ashes of a dead civilization.

Throughout Orwell's early novels, journals, and essays, democratic
socialism existed as a sustaining vision that kept the author from
total despair of the human condition, but Orwell's bitter experience
in the Spanish Civil War and the shock of the Nazi-Soviet pact sig-
naled the breakdown of this last hope and the beginning of the
mental and emotional state out of which grew *Animal Farm* and
*1984.* The political disappointments of the late '30s and '40s did not
in themselves, however, disillusion Orwell—they simply brought to
the surface themes and tensions present in his work from the beginning. As we observed earlier, the socialism Orwell believed in was

not a hardheaded, "realistic" approach to society and politics but a rather sentimental, utopian vision of the world as a "raft sailing through space, with, potentially, plenty of provisions for everybody," provided men, who, after all, are basically decent, would simply use common sense and not be greedy. Such naïve beliefs could only survive while Orwell was preoccupied with his attacks on the British Raj, the artist in society, or the capitalist system. The moment events compelled him to turn his critical eye on the myth of socialism and the "dictatorship of the proletariat," he discerned fundamental lies and corruption. Orwell, in his last years, was a man who experienced daily the disintegration of the beliefs of a lifetime, who watched in horror while his entire life work was robbed of meaning.

The first of his great cries of despair was *Animal Farm* (1946), a satirical beast fable which, curiously enough, has been heralded as Orwell's lightest, gayest work. Laurence Brander, in his biography of Orwell, paints a charming but wholly inaccurate picture of *Animal Farm*, presenting it as "one of those apparently chance pieces a prose writer throws off . . . a sport out of his usual way," supposedly written by Orwell in a state where "the gaiety in his nature had completely taken charge . . . writing about animals, whom he loved." [4] The surface gaiety, the seeming good humor and casualness, the light, bantering tone are, of course, part of the convention of beast fables, and *Animal Farm* would be a very bad tale indeed if it did not employ these devices. But it is a remarkable achievement precisely because Orwell uses the apparently frivolous form of the animal tale to convey with immense power his profoundly bitter message. Critics like Laurence Brander and Tom Hopkinson who marvel at Orwell's "admirable good humour and detachment" [5] miss, I think, the whole point of the piece they praise. *Animal Farm* does indeed contain much gaiety and humor, but even in the most comic moments there is a disturbing element of cruelty or fear that taints the reader's hearty laughter. While Snowball, one of the leaders of the revolution of farm animals against their master, is organizing "the Egg Production Committee for the hens, the

4 Laurence Brander, *George Orwell* (London, 1954), p. 171.
5 Hopkinson, p. 31.

Clean Tails League for the cows, the Wild Comrades' Re-education Committee . . . , the Whiter Wool Movement for the sheep," Napoleon the sinister pig tyrant, is carefully educating the dogs for his own evil purposes. Similarly, the "confessions" forced from the animals in Napoleon's great purges are very funny, but when the dogs tear the throats out of the "guilty" parties and leave a pile of corpses at the tyrant's feet, the scene ceases to amuse. Orwell's technique is similar to the device we have seen in Waugh, who relates ghastly events in a comic setting.

Another critical mistake in appraising *Animal Farm* is made, I believe, by critics like Christopher Hollis who talk of the overriding importance of the author's love of animals[6] and fail to understand that Orwell in *Animal Farm* loves animals only as much or as little as he loves human beings. To claim that he hates the pigs because they represent human tyrants and sympathizes with the horses because they are dumb animals is absurd. Nor is it necessary, as Hollis believes, that the truly successful animal fable carry with it "a gay and light-hearted message." [7] Indeed, the very idea of representing human traits in animals is rather pessimistic. What is essential to the success of the satirical beast fable, as Ellen Douglas Leyburn observes, is the author's power to keep his reader conscious simultaneously of the human traits satirized and of the animals as animals." [8] The storyteller must never allow the animals to be simply beasts, in which case the piece becomes a nonsatirical children's story, or to be merely transparent symbols, in which case the piece becomes a dull sermon. Orwell proved, in *Animal Farm*, his remarkable ability to maintain this delicate, satiric balance.

The beast fable, an ancient satiric technique in which the characteristic poses of human vice and folly are embodied in animals, is, as Kernan points out, "an unrealistic, expressionistic device" [9] which stands in bold contrast with Orwell's previous realistic manner. But the seeds for *Animal Farm* are present in the earlier works,

6 Hollis, p. 148.

7 Ibid., p. 147.

8 Ellen Douglass Leyburn, "Animal Stories," in *Modern Satire*, ed. Alvin Kernan (New York, 1962), p. 215.

9 "Introduction to Orwell's *Animal Farm*," in *Modern Satire*, p. 106.

not only in the metaphors likening men to beasts but, more important, in Orwell's whole attitude toward society, which he sees as an aggregation of certain classes or types. The types change somewhat in appearance according to the setting—from the snobbish pukka sahibs, corrupt officials, and miserable natives of *Burmese Days* to the obnoxious nouveaux riches, greedy restaurateurs, and overworked plongeurs of *Down and Out in Paris and London,* but there remains the basic notion that men naturally divide themselves into a limited number of groups, which can be isolated and characterized by the astute observer. This notion is given dramatic reality in *Animal Farm,* where societal types are presented in the various kinds of farm animals—pigs for exploiters, horses for laborers, dogs for police, sheep for blind followers, etc. The beast fable need not convey an optimistic moral, but it cannot portray complex individuals, and thus it can never sustain the burden of tragedy. The characters of a satirical animal story may be sly, vicious, cynical, pathetic, lovable, or intelligent, but they can only be seen as members of large social groups and not as individuals.

*Animal Farm* has been interpreted most frequently as a clever satire on the betrayal of the Russian Revolution and the rise of Stalin. Richard Rees comments that "the struggle of the farm animals, having driven out their human exploiter, to create a free and equal community takes the form of a most ingeniously worked-out recapitulation of the history of Soviet Russia from 1917 up to the Teheran Conference." [10] And indeed, despite Soviet critics who claim to see only a general satire on bureaucracy in *Animal Farm,* [11] the political allegory is inevitable. Inspired by the prophetic deathbed vision of Old Major, a prize Middle White boar, the maltreated animals of Manor Farm successfully revolt against Mr. Jones, their bad farmer, and found their own utopian community, Animal Farm. The control of the revolution falls naturally upon the pigs, particularly upon Napoleon, "a large, rather fierce-looking Berkshire boar, not much of a talker, but with a reputation for getting his own way," and on Snowball, "a more vivacious pig than Napoleon,

10 Rees, *George Orwell,* p. 84.
11 Hollis, p. 145.

quicker in speech and more inventive, but . . . not considered to
have the same depth of character." Under their clever leadership
and with the help of the indefatigable cart horses Boxer and Clover,
the animals manage to repulse the attacks of their rapacious human
neighbors, Mr. Pilkington and Mr. Frederick. With the farm secured
from invasion and the Seven Commandments of Animalism painted
on the end wall of the big barn, the revolution seems complete; but
as the community develops, it is plain that there are graver dangers
than invasion. The pigs at once decide that milk and apples are
essential to their well being. Squealer, Napoleon's lieutenant and
the ablest talker, explains the appropriation:

> "Comrades!" he cried. "You do not imagine, I hope, that we pigs
> are doing this in a spirit of selfishness and privilege? Many of us
> actually dislike milk and apples . . . Our sole object in taking these
> things is to preserve our health. Milk and apples (this has been
> proven by Science, comrades) contain substances absolutely necessary
> to the well-being of a pig . . . We pigs are brainworkers . . . Day
> and night we are watching over your welfare. It is for *your* sake that
> we drink that milk and eat those apples. Do you know what would
> happen if we pigs failed in our duty? Jones would come back!" [12]

A growing rivalry between Snowball and Napoleon is decisively
decided by Napoleon's vicious hounds, who drive Snowball off the
farm. Laurence Brander sees Snowball as a symbol of "altruism, the
essential social virtue" and his expulsion as the defeat of "his altruistic laws for giving warmth, food and comfort to all the animals."[13]
This is very touching, but unfortunately there is no indication that
Snowball is any less corrupt or power-mad than Napoleon. Indeed,
it is remarked, concerning the appropriation of the milk and apples,
that "All the pigs were in full agreement on this point, even Snowball and Napoleon" (p. 30). The remainder of *Animal Farm* is a
chronicle of the consolidation of Napoleon's power through clever
politics, propaganda, and terror. Dissenters are ruthlessly murdered,
and when Boxer can no longer work, he is sold to the knacker. One

12 Orwell, *Animal Farm* (New York, 1946), p. 30.
13 Brander, p. 175.

by one, the Commandments of Animalism are perverted or eliminated, until all that is left is:

ALL ANIMALS ARE EQUAL
BUT SOME ANIMALS ARE MORE EQUAL THAN OTHERS.

After that, it does not seem strange when the pigs live in Jones'
house, walk on two legs, carry whips, wear human clothes, take out
subscriptions to *John Bull, Tit-Bits,* and the *Daily Mirror,* and
invite their human neighbors over for a friendly game of cards. The
game ends in a violent argument when Napoleon and Pilkington
play an ace of spades simultaneously, but for the animals there is no
real quarrel. "The creatures outside looked from pig to man, and
from man to pig, and from pig to man again; but already it was
impossible to say which was which."

The interpretation of *Animal Farm* in terms of Soviet history
(Major, Napoleon, Snowball represent Lenin, Stalin, Trotsky) has
been made many times[14] and shall not be pursued further here. It is
amusing, however, that many of the Western critics who astutely
observe the barbs aimed at Russia fail completely to grasp Orwell's
judgment of the West. After all, the pigs do not turn into alien
monsters; they come to resemble those bitter rivals Mr. Pilkington
and Mr. Frederick, who represent the Nazis and the Capitalists. All
three major "powers" are despicable tyrannies, and the failure of
the revolution is not seen in terms of ideology at all, but as a realization of Lord Acton's thesis, "Power tends to corrupt; absolute
power corrupts absolutely." The initial spark of a revolution, the
original intention of a constitution may have been an ideal of the
good life, but the result is always the same—tyranny. Communism
is no more or less evil than Fascism or Capitalism—they are all
illusions which are inevitably used by the pigs as a means of satis-
fying their greed and their lust for power. Religion, too, is merely
a toy of the oppressors and a device to divert the minds of the suf-
ferers. Moses, the tame raven who is always croaking about the
sweet, eternal life in Sugarcandy Mountain, flies after the deposed

14 E.g. Hollis, p. 145.

Farmer Jones, only to return when Napoleon has established his tyranny.

*Animal Farm* remains powerful satire even as the specific historical events it mocked recede into the past, because the book's major concern is not with these incidents but with the essential horror of the human condition. There have been, are, and always will be pigs in every society, Orwell states, and they will always grab power. Even more cruel is the conclusion that *everyone* in the society, wittingly or unwittingly, contributes to the pigs' tyranny. Boxer, the noblest (though not the wisest) animal on the farm, devotes his unceasing labor to the pigs, who, as has been noted, send him to the knacker when he has outlived his usefulness. There is real pathos as the sound of Boxer's hoofs drumming weakly on the back of the horse slaughterer's van grows fainter and dies away, and the reader senses that in that dying sound is the dying hope of humanity. But Orwell does not allow the mood of oppressive sadness to overwhelm the satire, and Squealer, "lifting his trotter and wiping away a tear," hastens to announce that, after receiving every attention a horse could have, Boxer died in his hospital bed, with the words "Napoleon is always right" on his withered lips. Frederick R. Karl, in *The Contemporary English Novel,* believes that *Animal Farm* fails as successful satire "by virtue of its predictability," [15] but this terrifying predictability of the fate of all revolutions is just the point Orwell is trying to make. The grotesque end of the fable is not meant to shock the reader—indeed, chance and surprise are banished entirely from Orwell's world. The horror of both *Animal Farm* and the later *1984* is precisely the cold, orderly, predictable process by which decency, happiness, and hope are systematically and ruthlessly crushed.

*1984* (published in 1949) is Orwell's last novel, and it brings together every strand of his previous work. The black pessimism of this book may be, in part, explained by the fact that Orwell's wife had died suddenly in 1945, that his own health was deteriorating, that he sensed that he was dying, but the mood of suicidal despair

[15] Frederick R. Karl, *The Contemporary English Novel* (New York, 1959), p. 163.

which pervades *1984* seems even more to be the result of Orwell's conclusion that he had explored all the so-called solutions to man's misery and found nothing but lies. The whole world, Orwell felt, is steadily moving toward a vast and ruthless tyranny, and there is absolutely nothing that can stop the monstrous progress. *1984,* in spite of its setting in the future, is not primarily a utopian fantasy prophesying what the world will be like in thirty or forty years but a novel about what the world is like now. Hopkinson, discussing what he believes is the failure of *1984,* complains that "Orwell, sick and dispirited, has imagined nothing new . . . His world of *1984* is the war-time world of 1944, but dirtier and more cruel—and with all the endurance and nobility which distinguished mankind in that upheaval, mysteriously drained away. *Everyone* by *1984* is to be a coward, a spy, and a betrayer . . . The horror which distorts life in the future is merely the horror that hangs over life today." [16] It is difficult to respond to a critic like Mr. Hopkinson, for he denies the whole purpose of Orwell's novel, which is to show, by means of the expressionistic device of the utopian novel, "merely the horror that hangs over life today." The contemporary relevance is seen, of course, in the allegory of a world divided into three power blocs—Oceania, Eurasia, and Eastasia—which roughly resemble the present major powers; in the dominant ideology of Oceania, called Ingsoc, which is obviously an abbreviation of English Socialism: in the "history" of the first half of the twentieth century; and in the setting, which Hopkinson points out is so clearly London, 1944. This immediacy, however, is even more apparent in the major themes of the book, which have all been examined, in a more "realistic" context, in Orwell's earlier novels and essays—the disappearance of the heroic, the crushing of the individual, the cynical tampering with history, the contempt for liberty, the inevitable tyranny of the pigs, the physical horror of existence.

*1984* is the story of the revolt against society of one man, Winston Smith, but, as in all of Orwell's novels, the environment is far more important than the characters or the plot. The world against which Winston raises his feeble and doomed rebellion is a composite of

[16] Hopkinson, p. 35.

every hell Orwell ever attempted to portray. It is the dirty, ugly city George Bowling confronted in *Coming Up for Air,* the night-marish, savage jungle of *Burmese Days,* the squalid slums and doss houses of *Down and Out in Paris and London,* the gloomy subter-ranean chambers and smoking slag heaps of *The Road to Wigan Pier,* and, above all, the filthy prison-house world of "Such, Such Were the Joys . . ." The spirit of Oceania so closely resembles that of Crossgates school that Anthony West complained that "What Orwell did in *1984* was to send everybody in England to an enor-mous Crossgates to be as miserable as himself." [17] And indeed, the terrors and pains which afflict Winston Smith are remarkably like those experienced by the young child, overwhelmed by "a sense of desolate loneliness and helplessness, of being locked up not only in a hostile world but in a world of good and evil where the rules were such that it was actually not possible for me to keep them" ("Such, Such Were the Joys . . . ," p. 13). Orwell recalls that once, when he had broken school rules and bought some chocolates, he noticed a small, sharp-faced man staring very hard at his school cap and was convinced that this man was a spy placed there by Sim, the head-master: "It did not seem to me strange that the headmaster of a private school should dispose of an army of informers . . . Sim was all-powerful, and it was natural that his agents should be every-where" (p. 23). In the world of *1984* the tyrant, Big Brother, does employ a vast army of informers, called thought police, who watch every individual at all times for the least signs of criminal deviation, which may consist simply of unorthodox thoughts, let alone buying chocolates without orders.

In spite of the complex mythology of a savior-tyrant and the con-stant admonitions that "Big Brother Is Watching You," Oceania, like Eurasia and Eastasia, is ruled by a system of oligarchical col-lectivism, by an all-powerful Party, which has abolished private property and whose members are designated, according to their power and responsibility, Inner Party or Outer Party. The mem-bership of the Party is only 15 per cent of the population; the re-maining 85 per cent are the Proles, kept in a state of abject poverty

[17] West, quoted in Dooley, p. 293.

and total ignorance, "prolefed" lies by the Ministry of Truth, ter-
rorized by the Ministry of Love. The economy of Oceania is always
on an emergency basis, for there is perpetual war between the three
powers, not to win control of the disputed territory between them,
but deliberately to perpetuate shortages, to create a horribly low
standard of living that will keep the people miserable. As Orwell
learned in *Down and Out in Paris and London,* poverty eliminates
the possibility of thought, and independent thinking is the greatest
danger to the totalitarian states. The goal of the three powers, then,
is not victory but everlasting war, and though no contact of any kind
is allowed between the states, "as long as they remain in conflict
they prop one another up like three sheaves of corn." [18] War, therefore, is essential to the stability of the state, and thus the first basic
tenet of Oceania: War Is Peace.

The remaining principles of the totalitarian state are related to
Orwell's growing concern, in the last years of his life, with the relation between politics and language.[19] If language is abused, if words
can have entirely contradictory meanings at the same time, if the
language necessary to express political opposition is destroyed, if
notions of objective truth and unchanging history are abandoned,
then since thought is dependent on language, all unorthodox modes
of thought can be made impossible, history can be altered to suit
the needs of the moment, the individual can be reduced to an automaton, incapable of thought or disloyalty. Orwell found he could
not fully integrate into the plot of *1984* these rather complex reflections on the development of the modern state and its use of language, and so he wisely developed his ideas in two essays, the first
inserted in the novel as a heretical book entitled "The Theory and
Practice of Oligarchical Collectivism," reputedly by the archenemy
of the State, Emmanuel Goldstein, but actually written by the
thought police as a trap for Winston. The second essay is placed
outside the novel entirely as an Appendix entitled "The Principles
of Newspeak."

It is against a vast, ruthless, immensely powerful state that Winston Smith rebels. Like all of Orwell's heroes, Winston is neither

[18] Orwell, *1984* (New York, Signet Books, 1949), p. 150.
[19] See Orwell, "Politics and the English Language," *Essays,* pp. 162–77.

glorious, nor brave, nor resourceful, nor even truly rebellious. He is a smallish, frail figure, with a varicose ulcer above his right ankle, false teeth, and, of course, a hyper-developed sense of smell. He is frozen by the vile wind, sickened by the heavy odor of boiled cabbage and old rag mats in his hallway and the overpowering smell of sweat of his fat neighbor, nauseated by the regulation lunch— "a pinkish-gray . . . filthy liquid mess that had the appearance of vomit." Winston's revolt is not motivated primarily by love of freedom, belief in the dignity of man, or even sexual passion, but by a lack of discipline, a failure in his education. Like the little boy at Crossgates, he is unable to control his instincts and thus unable to be loyal. The dramatic tension of *1984* is not whether Winston will be able to revolt successfully against the Party, for such revolt is inconceivable. By means of a spying device called a telescreen, the thought police keep all Party members under constant surveillance, and Winston knows that he is doomed from the moment he has his first heretical thought. The tensions of the novel concern how long he can stay alive and whether it is possible for Winston to die without mentally betraying his rebellion.

Winston Smith's active revolt begins with his decision to keep a diary, but it receives its full expression in his love affair with Julia, a co-worker in the Ministry of Truth. Unlike Winston, Julia is not even vaguely interested in politics or ideology. Her heresy is "sex-crime"—she enjoys sexual intercourse. Sex, like the family, represents a threat to the state, because it is essentially private, isolated, uncontrollable. Through a great many maneuvers and subterfuges Winston and Julia manage secretly to arrange meetings and eventually to rent an apartment in a proletarian slum from an antique-shop owner named Charrington. The couple also make contact with O'Brien, a mysterious Inner Party member who tells them he is an agent of Goldstein and enlists them in a Brotherhood dedicated to the overthrow of the party. Winston had thought that the only hope for the overthrow of Big Brother lay in the proles, but O'Brien explains that "from the proletarians nothing is to be feared. Left to themselves, they will continue from generation to generation and from century to century, working, breeding, and dying, not only without any impulse to rebel, but without the power of grasping

that the world could be other than it is" (p. 160). If the proles are
useless, it is not clear how the Brotherhood will destroy the State,
but Winston and Julia promise, nonetheless, that they are fully
prepared, if called upon, to murder, to commit acts of sabotage, "to
cheat, to forge, to blackmail, to corrupt the minds of children, to
distribute habit-forming drugs, to encourage prostitution, to dis-
seminate venereal diseases. . . . to throw sulphuric acid in a child's
face" (p. 131). It is clear, of course, that even if there were a Brotherhood based on these pinciples, it could only replace the tyranny of
Big Brother with another as evil. The possibility is never explored,
however, because both Charrington and O'Brien are members of
the thought police, the Brotherhood is merely a trap, and Winston
and Julia are arrested.

The remainder of *1984* is a record of the total annihilation of
Winston Smith, the destruction of his personality, his "reintegra-
tion" into society, under the cruel but steady hand of O'Brien. It
becomes increasingly apparent in the course of the novel that Big
Brother is a surrogate God and that the members of the Inner Party
are His priests, and so it is not surprising that O'Brien takes on the
role of inquisitor whose duty is to purify Winston by exorcising the
demon of heresy. Within this religious context Winston can finally
receive the answer to his gnawing question—*Why* does the Party
cling to power? Just as in *Keep the Aspidistra Flying,* "money" was
substituted for "charity" in the passage from St. Paul, so, in *1984,*
"power" is substituted for "God." "God is Power" is the final revela-
tion of *1984,* and thus O'Brien's answer to Winston's "Why?" is
simple:

> The Party seeks power entirely for its own sake. We are not inter-
> ested in the good of others; we are interested solely in power. Not
> wealth or luxury or long life or happiness; only power, pure power.
> . . . The object of power is power. . . . The world that we are pre-
> paring [is] a world of victory after victory, triumph after triumph
> after triumph: an endless pressing, pressing, pressing upon the nerve
> of power.      [pp. 200–204]

O'Brien and his colleagues are not men but embodiments of the
power principle who, as D. J. Dooley points out, "achieve a vicarious

immortality through membership in the Inner Party, since the mind of the Party is collective and immortal." [20]

Winston Smith represents the spirit of man in *1984,* but, as O'Brien relentlessly strips away man's protective clothing, the robes of civilization and culture, the garments of refinement, health, and common sense, the human being is revealed to be nothing more than a vile "bag of filth" (p. 207). The description of Winston Smith, dirty, rotting, emaciated, stinking like a goat, confronting himself in a mirror in the Ministry of Love, recalls Swift's description of the revolting Yahoos in *Gulliver's Travels.* Man is repulsive, ugly, stupid, cowardly, filthy, and disgusting. Orwell's triumphant humanism has been destroyed, and all that is left is the final vision of Winston, having betrayed Julia and himself, waiting for the bullet that will end his miserable life, drinking foul gin, crying miserable tears of repentance, loving Big Brother.

One wonders what Orwell would have written after *1984.* Evelyn Waugh found Catholicism and Aldous Huxley discovered his perennial philosophy after *Brave New World* and *Ape and Essence,* but somehow one cannot imagine George Orwell settling back into a warm and cozy orthodoxy of his own. At any rate, Orwell precluded this possibility by moving, against his doctors' orders, to the rough island of Jura in the Inner Hebrides, where his chronic cough developed into tuberculosis. He died in London in January 1950, at the age of 47.

Orwell could never bring himself to say "I accept" in "an epoch of fear, tyranny, and regimentation," an age of:

> concentration camps, rubber truncheons, Hitler, Stalin, bombs, aeroplanes, tinned food, machine guns, putsches, purges, slogans, Bedaux belts, gas masks, submarines, spies, provocateurs, press censorship, secret prisons, aspirins, Hollywood films, and political murders.[21]

Orwell was unwilling, indeed one senses that he was totally unable to resign himself quietly to the grim necessity of such a catalogue of horrors in human society. Desperately, he sought an alternative, an instrument of change, a means of relief, but his keen perception of

20 Dooley, p. 298.
21 Orwell, "Inside the Whale," *Essays,* p. 223.

hypocrisy and fraud, his unfailing hatred of injustice and tyranny, his morbidly sensitive nose for rottenness and the vile smells of humanity systematically destroyed every system, every ideology, every code that presented itself as a palliative for man's suffering. Orwell's work is the unspeakably sad record of a completely up-rooted individual, a man plagued by fundamental moral confusion, driven by a passion for clarity and certainty in a hopelessly confused society, tormented by the burning need for personal commitment in a world where worth-while causes had ceased to exist.

# 1984—The Mysticism of Cruelty

## by Isaac Deutscher

Few novels written in this generation have obtained a popularity as great as that of George Orwell's *1984*. Few, if any, have made a similar impact on politics. The title of Orwell's book is a political by-word. The terms coined by him—"Newspeak," "Oldspeak," "Mutability of the Past," "Big Brother," "Ministry of Truth," "Thought Police," "Crimethink," "Doublethink," "Hateweek," etc.—have entered the political vocabulary; they occur in most newspaper articles and speeches denouncing Russia and communism. Television and the cinema have familiarized many millions of viewers on both sides of the Atlantic with the menacing face of Big Brother and the nightmare of a supposedly communist Oceania. The novel has served as a sort of an ideological super-weapon in the cold war. As in no other book or document, the convulsive fear of communism, which has swept the West since the end of the Second World War, has been reflected and focused in *1984*.

The cold war has created a "social demand" for such an ideological weapon just as it creates the demand for physical super-weapons. But the super-weapons are genuine feats of technology; and there can be no discrepancy between the uses to which they may be put and the intention of their producers: they are meant to spread death or at least to threaten utter destruction. A book like *1984* may be used without much regard for the author's intention. Some of its features may be torn out of their context, while others,

"*1984*—The Mysticism of Cruelty." From *Heretics and Renegades*, by Isaac Deutscher, written in December 1954 (London: Hamish Hamilton Ltd., 1956). Reprinted by permission of Jonathan Cape Ltd., and The Bobbs-Merrill Company, Inc.

which do not suit the political purpose which the book is made to serve, are ignored or virtually suppressed. Nor need a book like *1984* be a literary masterpiece or even an important and original work to make its impact. Indeed a work of great literary merit is usually too rich in its texture and too subtle in thought and form to lend itself to adventitious exploitation. As a rule, its symbols cannot easily be transformed into hypnotizing bogies, or its ideas turned into slogans. The words of a great poet when they enter the political vocabulary do so by a process of slow, almost imperceptible infiltration, not by a frantic incursion. The literary masterpiece influences the political mind by fertilizing and enriching it from the inside, not by stunning it.

*1984* is the work of an intense and concentrated, but also fear-ridden and restricted imagination. A hostile critic has dismissed it as a "political horror-comic." This is not a fair description: there are in Orwell's novel certain layers of thought and feeling which raise it well above that level. But it is a fact that the symbolism of *1984* is crude; that its chief symbol, Big Brother, resembles the bogy-man of a rather inartistic nursery tale; and that Orwell's story unfolds like the plot of a science-fiction film of the cheaper variety, with mechanical horror piling up upon mechanical horror so much that, in the end, Orwell's subtler ideas, his pity for his characters, and his satire on the society of his own days (not of 1984) may fail to communicate themselves to the reader. *1984* does not seem to justify the description of Orwell as the modern Swift, a description for which *Animal Farm* provides some justification. Orwell lacks the richness and subtlety of thought and the philosophical detachment of the great satirist. His imagination is ferocious and at times penetrating, but it lacks width, suppleness, and originality.

The lack of originality is illustrated by the fact that Orwell borrowed the idea of *1984,* the plot, the chief characters, the symbols, and the whole climate of his story from a Russian writer who has remained almost unknown in the West. That writer is Evgenii Zamyatin, and the title of the book which served Orwell as the model is *We.* Like *1984, We* is an "anti-Utopia," a nightmare vision of the shape of things to come, and a Cassandra cry. Orwell's work is a thoroughly English variation on Zamyatin's theme; and it is perhaps only the thoroughness of Orwell's English approach that gives to his work the originality that it possesses.

A few words about Zamyatin may not be out of place here: there are some points of resemblance in the life stories of the two writers. Zamyatin belonged to an older generation: he was born in 1884 and died in 1937. His early writings, like some of Orwell's, were realistic descriptions of the lower middle class. In his experience the Russian revolution of 1905 played approximately the same role that the Spanish civil war played in Orwell's. He participated in the revolutionary movement, was a member of the Russian Social Democratic Party (to which Bolsheviks and Mensheviks then still belonged), and was persecuted by the Tsarist police. At the ebb of the revolution, he succumbed to a mood of "cosmic pessimism"; and he severed his connection with the Socialist Party, a thing which Orwell, less consistent and to the end influenced by a lingering loyalty to socialism, did not do. In 1917 Zamyatin viewed the new revolution with cold and disillusioned eyes, convinced that nothing good would come out of it. After a brief imprisonment, he was allowed by the Bolshevik government to go abroad; and it was as an émigré in Paris that he wrote *We* in the early 1920's.

The assertion that Orwell borrowed the main elements of *1984* from Zamyatin is not the guess of a critic with a foible for tracing literary influences. Orwell knew Zamyatin's novel and was fascinated by it. He wrote an essay about it, which appeared in the left-socialist *Tribune,* of which Orwell was Literary Editor, on 4 January 1946, just after the publication of *Animal Farm* and before he began writing *1984.* The essay is remarkable not only as a conclusive piece of evidence, supplied by Orwell himself, on the origin of *1984,* but also as a commentary on the idea underlying both *We* and *1984.*

The essay begins with Orwell saying that after having for years looked in vain for Zamyatin's novel, he had at last obtained it in a French edition (under the title *Nous Autres*), and that he was surprised that it had not been published in England, although an American edition had appeared without arousing much interest. "So far as I can judge," Orwell went on, "it is not a book of the first order, but it is certainly an unusual one, and it is astonishing that no English publisher has been enterprising enough to re-issue it." (He concluded the essay with the words: "This is a book to look out for when an English version appears.")

Orwell noticed that Aldous Huxley's *Brave New World* "must be partly derived" from Zamyatin's novel and wondered why this had "never been pointed out." Zamyatin's book was, in his view, much superior and more "relevant to our own situation" than Huxley's. It dealt "with the rebellion of the primitive human spirit against a rationalized, mechanized, painless world."

"Painless" is not the right adjective: the world of Zamyatin's vision is as full of horrors as is that of *1984*. Orwell himself produced in his essay a succinct catalogue of those horrors so that his essay reads now like a synopsis of *1984*. The members of the society described by Zamyatin, says Orwell, "have so completely lost their individuality as to be known only by numbers. They live in glass houses . . . which enables the political police, known as the 'guardians', to supervise them more easily. They all wear identical uniforms, and a human being is commonly referred to either as 'a number' or a 'unif' (uniform)." Orwell remarks in parentheses that Zamyatin wrote "before television was invented." In *1984* this technological refinement is brought in as well as the helicopters from which the police supervise the homes of the citizens of Oceania in the opening passages of the novel. The "unifs" suggest the "Proles." In Zamyatin's society of the future as in *1984* love is forbidden: sexual intercourse is strictly rationed and permitted only as an unemotional act. "The Single State is ruled over by a person known as the Benefactor," the obvious prototype of Big Brother.

"The guiding principle of the State is that happiness and freedom are incompatible . . . the Single State has restored his [man's] happiness by removing his freedom." Orwell describes Zamyatin's chief character as "a sort of Utopian Billy Brown of London town" who is "constantly horrified by the atavistic impulses which seize upon him." In Orwell's novel that Utopian Billy Brown is christened Winston Smith, and his problem is the same.

For the main *motif* of his plot Orwell is similarly indebted to the Russian writer. This is how Orwell defines it: "In spite of education and the vigilance of the Guardians, many of the ancient human instincts are still there." Zamyatin's chief character "falls in love (this is a crime, of course) with a certain I-330" just as Winston Smith commits the crime of falling in love with Julia. In Zamyatin's as in Orwell's story the love affair is mixed up with the hero's participation in an "underground resistance movement." Zamyatin's rebels "apart from plotting the overthrow of the State, even indulge, at the moment when their curtains are down, in such vices as smoking cigarettes and drinking alcohol"; Winston Smith and Julia indulge in drinking "real coffee with real sugar" in their hideout over Mr. Charrington's shop. In both novels the crime and the conspiracy are, of course, discovered by the Guardians or the Thought Police; and in both the hero "is ultimately saved from the consequences of his own folly."

The combination of "cure" and torture by which Zamyatin's and Orwell's rebels are "freed" from the atavistic impulses, until they begin to love Benefactor or Big Brother, are very much the same. In Zamyatin: "The authorities announce that they have discovered the cause of the recent disorders: it is that some human beings suffer from a disease called imagination. The nerve centre responsible for imagination has now been located, and the disease can be cured by X-ray treatment. D-503 undergoes the operation, after which it is easy for him to do what he has known all along that he ought to do—that is, betray his confederates to the police." In both novels the act of confession and the betrayal of the woman the hero loves are the curative shocks.

Orwell quotes the following scene of torture from Zamyatin:

> She looked at me, her hands clasping the arms of the chair, until her eyes were completely shut. They took her out, brought her to herself by means of an electric shock, and put her under the bell again. This operation was repeated three times, and not a word issued from her lips.

In Orwell's scenes of torture the "electric shocks" and the "arms of the chair" recur quite often, but Orwell is far more intense, masochistic-sadistic, in his descriptions of cruelty and pain. For instance:

Without any warning except a slight movement of O'Brien's hand, a wave of pain flooded his body. It was a frightening pain, because he could not see what was happening, and he had the feeling that some mortal injury was being done to him. He did not know whether the thing was really happening, or whether the effect was electrically produced; but his body had been wrenched out of shape, the joints were being slowly torn apart. Although the pain had brought the sweat out on his forehead, the worst of all was the fear that his backbone was about to snap. He set his teeth and breathed hard through his nose, trying to keep silent as long as possible.

The list of Orwell's borrowings is far from complete; but let us now turn from the plot of the two novels to their underlying idea. Taking up the comparison between Zamyatin and Huxley, Orwell says: "It is this intuitive grasp of the irrational side of totalitarianism—human sacrifice, cruelty as an end in itself, the worship of a Leader who is credited with divine attributes—that makes Zamyatin's book superior to Huxley's." It is this, we may add, that made of it Orwell's model. Criticizing Huxley, Orwell writes that he could find no clear reason why the society of *Brave New World* should be so rigidly and elaborately stratified: "The aim is not economic exploitation. . . . *There is no power-hunger, no sadism, no hardness of any kind.* Those at the top have no strong motive for staying on the top, and though everyone is happy in a vacuous way, life has become so pointless that it is difficult to believe that such a society could endure." (My italics.) In contrast, the society of Zamyatin's anti-Utopia could endure, in Orwell's view, because in it the supreme motive of action and the reason for social stratification are not economic exploitation, for which there is no need, but precisely the "power-hunger, sadism, and hardness" of those who "stay at the top." It is easy to recognize in this the *leitmotif* of *1984*.

In Oceania technological development has reached so high a level that society could well satisfy all its material needs and establish equality in its midst. But inequality and poverty are maintained in order to keep Big Brother in power. In the past, says Orwell, dictatorship safeguarded inequality, now safeguards dictatorship. But what purpose does the dictatorship itself serve? "The party seeks power entirely for its own sake. . . . Power is not a means, it is an end. One does not establish a dictatorship in order to safeguard a revolution; one makes the revolution in order to establish the dictatorship. The object of persecution is persecution. . . . The object of power is power."

Orwell wondered whether Zamyatin did "intend the Soviet régime to be the special target of his satire." He was not sure of this: "What Zamyatin seems to be aiming at is not any particular country but the implied aims of the industrial civilization. . . . It is evident from *We* that he had a strong leaning towards primitivism. . . . *We* is in effect a study of the Machine, the genie that man has thoughtlessly let out of its bottle and cannot put back again." The same ambiguity of the author's aim is evident also in *1984*.

Orwell's guess about Zamyatin was correct. Though Zamyatin was opposed to the Soviet régime, it was not exclusively, or even mainly, that régime which he satirized. As Orwell rightly remarked, the early Soviet Russia had few features in common with the super-mechanized State of Zamyatin's anti-Utopia. That writer's leaning towards primitivism was in line with a Russian tradition, with Slavophilism and hostility towards the bourgeois West, with the glorification of the *muzhik* and of the old patriarchal Russia, with Tolstoy and Dostoyevsky. Even as an émigré, Zamyatin was disillusioned with the West in the characteristically Russian fashion. At times he seemed half-reconciled with the Soviet régime when it was already producing its Benefactor in the person of Stalin. In so far as he directed the darts of his satire against Bolshevism, he did so on the ground that Bolshevism was bent on replacing the old primitive Russia by the modern, mechanized society. Curiously enough, he set his story in the year 2600; and he seemed to say to the Bolsheviks: this is what Russia will look like if you succeed in giving to your régime the background of Western technology. In Zamyatin, like in some other Russian intellectuals disillusioned with socialism, the hankering after the primitive modes of thought and life was in so far natural as primitivism was still strongly alive in the Russian background.

In Orwell there was and there could be no such authentic nostalgia after the pre-industrial society. Primitivism had no part in his experience and background, except during his stay in Burma, when he was hardly attracted by it. But he was terrified of the uses to which technology might be put by men determined to enslave society; and so he, too, came to question and satirize "the implied aims of industrial civilization."

Although his satire is more recognizably aimed at Soviet Russia than Zamyatin's, Orwell saw elements of Oceania in the England of his own days as well, not to speak of the United States. Indeed, the society of *1984* embodies all that he hated and disliked in his own surroundings: the drabness and monotony of the English industrial suburb, the "filthy and grimy and smelly" ugliness of which he tried to match in his naturalistic, repetitive, and oppressive style; the food rationing and the government controls which he knew in war-time Britain; the "rubbishy newspapers containing almost nothing except sport, crime, and astrology, sensational five-cent novelettes, films oozing with sex"; and so on. Orwell knew well that newspapers of this sort did not exist in Stalinist Russia, and that the faults of the Stalinist Press were of an altogether different kind. *Newspeak* is much less a satire on the Stalinist idiom than on Anglo-American journalistic "cablese," which he loathed and with which, as a working journalist, he was well familiar.

It is easy to tell which features of the party of *1984* satirize the British Labor Party rather than the Soviet Communist Party. Big Brother and his followers make no attempt to indoctrinate the working class, an omission Orwell would have been the last to ascribe to Stalinism. His Proles "vegetate": "heavy work, petty quarrels, films, gambling . . . fill their mental horizon." Like the rubbishy newspapers and the films oozing with sex, so gambling, the new opium of the people, does not belong to the Russian scene. The Ministry of Truth is a transparent caricature of London's war-time Ministry of Information. The monster of Orwell's vision is, like every nightmare, made up of all sorts of faces and features and shapes, familiar and unfamiliar. Orwell's talent and originality are evident in the domestic aspect of his satire. But in the vogue which *1984* has enjoyed that aspect has rarely been noticed.

*1984* is a document of dark disillusionment not only with Stalinism but with every form and shade of socialism. It is a cry from the abyss of despair. What plunged Orwell into that abyss? It was without any doubt the spectacle of the Stalinist Great Purges of 1936–8, the repercussions of which he experienced in Catalonia. As a man of sensitivity and integrity, he could not react to the purges otherwise than with anger and horror. His conscience could not be soothed by the Stalinist justifications and sophisms which at the time did soothe the conscience of, for instance, Arthur Koestler, a writer of greater brilliance and sophistication but of less moral resolution. The Stalinist justifications and sophisms were both *beneath* and *above* Orwell's level of reasoning—they were beneath and above the common sense and the stubborn empiricism of Billy Brown of London town, with whom Orwell identified himself even in his most rebellious or revolutionary moments. He was outraged, shocked, and shaken in his beliefs. He had never been a member of the Communist Party. But, as an adherent of the semi-Trotskyist P.O.U.M., he had, despite all his reservations, tacitly assumed a certain community of purpose and solidarity with the Soviet régime through all its vicissitudes and transformations, which were to him somewhat obscure and exotic.

The purges and their Spanish repercussions not only destroyed that community of purpose. Not only did he see the gulf between Stalinists and anti-Stalinists opening suddenly inside embattled Republican Spain. This, the immediate effect of the purges, was overshadowed by "the irrational side of totalitarianism—human sacrifice, cruelty as an end in itself, the worship of a Leader," and "the colour of the sinister slave-civilizations of the ancient world" spreading over contemporary society.

Like most British socialists, Orwell had never been a Marxist. The dialectical-materialist philosophy had always been too abstruse for him. From instinct rather than consciousness he had been a staunch rationalist. The distinction between the Marxist and the rationalist is of some importance. Contrary to an opinion widespread in Anglo-Saxon countries, Marxism is not at all rationalist in its philosophy: it does not assume that human beings are, as a rule, guided by rational motives and that they can be argued into socialism by reason. Marx himself begins *Das Kapital* with the elaborate philosophical and historical inquiry into the "fetishistic" modes of thought and behavior rooted in "commodity production" —that is, in man's work for, and dependence on, a market. The class struggle, as Marx describes it, is anything but a rational process. This does not prevent the rationalists of socialism describing themselves sometimes as Marxists. But the authentic Marxist may claim to be mentally better prepared than the rationalist is for the manifestations of irrationality in human affairs, even for such manifestations as Stalin's Great Purges. He may feel upset or mortified by them, but he need not feel shaken in his *Weltanschauung*, while the rationalist is lost and helpless when the irrationality of the human existence suddenly stares him in the face. If he clings to his rationalism, reality eludes him. If he pursues reality and tries to grasp it, he must part with his rationalism.

Orwell pursued reality and found himself bereft of his conscious and unconscious assumptions about life. In his thoughts he could not henceforth get away from the Purges. Directly and indirectly, they supplied the subject matter for nearly all that he wrote after his Spanish experience. This was an honorable obsession, the obsession of a mind not inclined to cheat itself comfortably and to stop grappling with an alarming moral problem. But grappling with the Purges, his mind became infected by their irrationality. He found himself incapable of explaining what was happening in terms which were familiar to him, the terms of empirical common sense. Abandoning rationalism, he increasingly viewed reality through the dark glasses of a quasi-mystical pessimism.

It has been said that *1984* is the figment of the imagination of a dying man. There is some truth in this, but not the whole truth. It was indeed with the last feverish flicker of life in him that Orwell wrote this book. Hence the extraordinary, gloomy intensity of his vision and language, and the almost physical immediacy with which he suffered the tortures which his creative imagination was inflicting on his chief character. He identified his own withering physical existence with the decayed and shrunken body of Winston Smith, to whom he imparted and in whom he invested, as it were, his own dying pangs. He projected the last spasms of his own suffering into the last pages of his last book. But the main explanation of the inner logic of Orwell's disillusionment and pessimism lies not in the writer's death agonies, but in the experience and the thought of the living man and in his convulsive reaction from his defeated rationalism.

"I understand HOW: I do not understand WHY" is the refrain of *1984*. Winston Smith knows how Oceania functions and how its elaborate mechanism of tyranny works, but he does not know what is its ultimate cause and ultimate purpose. He turns for the answer to the pages of *"the* book," the mysterious classic of *crimethink,* the authorship of which is attributed to Emmanuel Goldstein, the inspirer of the conspiratorial Brotherhood. But he manages to read through only those chapters of *"the* book" which deal with the HOW. The Thought Police descend upon him just when he is about to begin reading the chapters which promise to explain WHY; and so the question remains unanswered.

This was Orwell's own predicament. He asked the Why not so much about the Oceania of his vision as about Stalinism and the Great Purges. At one point he certainly turned for the answer to Trotsky: it was from Trotsky-Bronstein that he took the few sketchy biographical data and even the physiognomy and the Jewish name for Emmanuel Goldstein; and the fragments of *"the* book," which take up so many pages in *1984,* are an obvious, though not very successful, paraphrase of Trotsky's *The Revolution Betrayed.* Orwell was impressed by Trotsky's moral grandeur and at the same time he partly distrusted it and partly doubted its authenticity. The ambivalence of his view of Trotsky finds its counterpart in Winston Smith's attitude towards Goldstein. To the end Smith cannot find out whether Goldstein and the Brotherhood have ever existed in reality, and whether *"the* book" was not concocted by the Thought Police. The barrier between Trotsky's thought and himself, a barrier which Orwell could never break down, was Marxism and dialectical materialism. He found in Trotsky the answer to How, not to Why.

But Orwell could not content himself with historical agnosticism. He was anything but a sceptic. His mental make-up was rather that of the fanatic, determined to get an answer, a quick and a plain answer, to his question. He was now tense with distrust and sus-

picion and on the look-out for the dark conspiracies hatched by
*them* against the decencies of Billy Brown of London town. *They*
were the Nazis, the Stalinists, and—Churchill and Roosevelt, and
ultimately all who had any *raison d'état* to defend, for at heart
Orwell was a simple-minded anarchist and, in his eyes, any political
movement forfeited its *raison d'être* the moment it acquired a
*raison d'état*. To analyze a complicated social background, to
try and unravel tangles of political motives, calculations, fears
and suspicions, and to discern the compulsion of circumstances
behind *their* action was beyond him. Generalizations about social forces, social trends, and historic inevitabilities made him
bristle with suspicion. Yet, without some such generalizations,
properly and sparingly used, no realistic answer could be given
to the question which preoccupied Orwell. His gaze was fixed
on the trees, or rather on a single tree, in front of him, and he
was almost blind to the wood. Yet his distrust of historical generalizations led him in the end to adopt and to cling to the oldest,
the most banal, the most abstract, the most metaphysical, and the
most barren of all generalizations: all *their* conspiracies and plots
and purges and diplomatic deals had one source and one source
only—"sadistic power-hunger." Thus he made his jump from
workaday, rationalistic common sense to the mysticism of cruelty
which inspires *1984*.[1]

1 This opinion is based on personal reminiscences as well as on an analysis of
Orwell's work. During the last war Orwell seemed attracted by the critical, then
somewhat unusual, tenor of my commentaries on Russia which appeared in *The
Economist, The Observer,* and *Tribune.* (Later we were both *The Observer's*
correspondents in Germany and occasionally shared a room in a Press camp.)
However, it took me little time to become aware of the differences of approach
behind our seeming agreement. I remember that I was taken aback by the stub-
bornness with which Orwell dwelt on "conspiracies," and that his political reasoning struck me as a Freudian sublimation of persecution mania. He was, for instance, unshakably convinced that Stalin, Churchill, and Roosevelt consciously
plotted to divide the world, and to divide it for good, among themselves, and to
subjugate it in common. (I can trace the idea of Oceania, Eastasia, and Eurasia
back to that time.) "*They* are all power-hungry," he used to repeat. When once
I pointed out to him that underneath the apparent solidarity of the Big Three
one could discern clearly the conflict between them, already coming to the surface, Orwell was so startled and incredulous that he at once related our conversation in his column in *Tribune,* and added that he saw no sign of the approach
of the conflict of which I spoke. This was by the time of the Yalta conference,

In *1984* man's mastery over the machine has reached so high a level that society is in a position to produce plenty for everybody and put an end to inequality. But poverty and inequality are maintained only to satisfy the sadistic urges of Big Brother. Yet we do not even know whether Big Brother really exists—he may be only a myth. It is the collective cruelty of the party (not necessarily of its individual members who may be intelligent and well-meaning people), that torments Oceania. Totalitarian society is ruled by a disembodied sadism. Orwell imagined that he had "transcended" the familiar and, as he thought, increasingly irrelevant concepts of social class and class interest. But in these Marxist generalizations, the interest of a social class bears at least some specific relation to the individual interests and the social position of its members, even if the class interest does not represent a simple sum of the individual interests. In Orwell's party the whole bears no relation to the parts. The party is not a social body actuated by any interest or purpose. It is a phantom-like emanation of all that is foul in human nature. It is the metaphysical, mad and triumphant, Ghost of Evil.

Of course, Orwell intended *1984* as a warning. But the warning defeats itself because of its underlying boundless despair. Orwell saw totalitarianism as bringing history to a standstill. Big Brother is invincible: "If you want a picture of the future, imagine a boot stamping on a human face—for ever." He projected the spectacle of the Great Purges on to the future, and he saw it fixed there for ever, because he was not capable of grasping the events realistically, in their complex historical context. To be sure, the events were highly "irrational"; but he who because of this treats them irrationally is very much like the psychiatrist whose mind becomes unhinged by dwelling too closely with insanity. *1984* is in effect not so much a warning as a piercing shriek announcing the advent of the Black Millennium, the Millennium of damnation.

The shriek, amplified by all the "mass-media" of our time, has

or shortly thereafter, when not much foresight was needed to see what was coming. What struck me in Orwell was his lack of historical sense and of psychological insight into political life coupled with an acute, though narrow, penetration into some aspects of politics and with an incorruptible firmness of conviction.

frightened millions of people. But it has not helped them to see more clearly the issues with which the world is grappling; it has not advanced their understanding. It has only increased and intensified the waves of panic and hate that run through the world and obfuscate innocent minds. *1984* has taught millions to look at the conflict between East and West in terms of black and white, and it has shown them a monster bogy and a monster scapegoat for all the ills that plague mankind.

At the onset of the atomic age, the world is living in a mood of Apocalyptic horror. That is why millions of people respond so passionately to the Apocalyptic vision of a novelist. The Apocalyptic atomic and hydrogen monsters, however, have not been let loose by Big Brother. The chief predicament of contemporary society is that it has not yet succeeded in adjusting its way of life and its social and political institutions to the prodigious advance of its technological knowledge. We do not know what has been the impact of the atomic and hydrogen bombs on the thoughts of millions in the East, where anguish and fear may be hidden behind the façade of a facile (or perhaps embarrassed?) official optimism. But it would be dangerous to blind ourselves to the fact that in the West millions of people may be inclined, in their anguish and fear, to flee from their own responsibility for mankind's destiny and to vent their anger and despair on the giant Bogy-cum-Scapegoat which Orwell's *1984* has done so much to place before their eyes.

*       *       *

"Have you read this book? You must read it, sir. Then you will know why we must drop the atom bomb on the Bolshies!" With these words a blind, miserable newsvendor recommended to me *1984* in New York, a few weeks before Orwell's death.

Poor Orwell, could he ever imagine that his own book would become so prominent an item in the programme of Hate Week?

# Orwell's Post-War Prophecy

## by Jenni Calder

There had been hints of *Nineteen Eighty-Four* in the very beginning of Orwell's writing career. Most of the themes had preoccupied him from about 1942. The book is a sign of the intensity with which he reacted against both the conditions of post-war Britain and the deadlock of the international situation. It is also an accumulation of all those aspects of life that Orwell felt most desperately about. A further consideration is the effect his illness was having on him, for the years in which he was writing *Nineteen Eighty-Four* were also the years in which his illness was at its most serious and debilitating.

The emotions and attitudes of the book had been present for many years, certainly present in *Wigan Pier* and *Keep the Aspidistra Flying,* if not earlier. He mentioned in his wartime Notebooks his long-held belief that the future would be "catastrophic," and it was clear throughout the War that he saw the future in extreme terms. He continually warned against complacency about totalitarianism: "the fallacy is to believe that under a dictatorial government you can be quite free *inside.* Quite a number of people console themselves with this thought, now that totalitarianism in one form or another is visibly on the upgrade in every part of the world." And in 1945 he prophesied the development which is the heart of *Nineteen Eighty-Four*:

> . . . We have before us the prospect of two or three monstrous super-States, each possessed of a weapon by which millions of people can be wiped out in a few seconds, dividing the world between them. It

"Orwell's Post-War Prophecy." From *Chronicles of Conscience,* by Jenni Calder (London: Secker and Warburg Ltd., 1968). Reprinted by permission of A D Peters and Company.

has been rather hastily assumed that that means bigger and bloodier wars, and perhaps an actual end to the machine civilisation. But suppose—and really this is the likelier development—that the surviving great nations made a tacit agreement never to use the atomic bomb against one another? Suppose they only use it, or the threat of it, against people who are unable to retaliate? In that case we are back where we were before, the only difference being that power is concentrated in still fewer hands and that the outlook for subject peoples and oppressed classes is still more hopeless.

This vision was not entirely Orwell's own. James Burnham predicted much the same development in *The Managerial Revolution,* a book whose assumptions Orwell disagreed with, yet which contained a number of ideas he admired. By the time *Nineteen Eighty-Four* was published the cold war was a reality, and Orwell's description of the politics of power blocs was extraordinarily apt.

There had, of course, been other anti-utopian works of fiction before *Nineteen Eighty-Four.* In January 1946 Orwell had written a short piece in *Tribune* on Eugene Zamyatin's book *We,* which he had read in a French edition. The book had been written in 1920 by a Russian exile. It was a prophecy of totalitarianism based on, Orwell thought, "not any particular country but the implied aims of industrial civilisation." Orwell was impressed by the book because its concept of totalitarianism was founded on what he considered an essential element of the dictatorial state. Zamyatin, he says, had "an intuitive grasp of the irrational side of totalitarianism—human sacrifice, cruelty as an end in itself, the worship of a Leader who is credited with divine attributes." This concept became an essential part of the creed of Ingsoc. It was a concept that Orwell had clearly been helped to formulate by Koestler's *Darkness At Noon* and Jack London's *The Iron Heel.* It was the aspect of the totalitarian state that was most difficult to combat. It could not be answered with intellectual argument, and its very nature tended to overwhelm logical explanation. Koestler, in fact, did not really attempt to explain or even to present the divinity of No. 1.

The events in *Darkness At Noon* take on the aura of ritual, but it is a ritual of the mind, not of the emotions. There is no cruelty for its own sake—this we tend to associate more with the Nazi régime—nor emotional build-up of the infallibility of No. 1. Yet the possibility is suggested. In *The Iron Heel* the Oligarchy's grasping for material wealth is transformed into a lust for power for its own sake, and the people's demands for social justice become an uncontrolled passion for revenge. Both these portrayals helped to form Orwell's understanding of authoritarian rule.

There is little indication that Orwell derived any wider influence from Zamyatin's book, although he greatly admired its ingenuity. *We* is constructed through a series of impressionistic pictures, studded with glittering detail, but leaving a sense of incompleteness. We get a sharp impression of contrast between the clean, bright city, built almost entirely of glass, and the slave-like existence of its inhabitants. Life is not dirty and colorless as in *Nineteen Eighty-Four,* but it is organized out of all humanity. The revolt in *We* is haphazard and imprecise. There are no explanations; we do not understand how it happens. Its aims and its inspiration are unclear; the impressionistic style ceases to be satisfactory. The mood and tone of *We* is far removed from *Nineteen Eighty-Four.* In its details it is far more distant from contemporary reality, particularly from Russia immediately after the Revolution. Its purpose appears to be much less particular, even less deliberate, than Orwell's.

But as a description of a dictatorial society Orwell found *We* much more satisfactory than Huxley's *Brave New World,* published in 1930. His chief criticism was that *Brave New World's* ruling group had neither energy nor purpose:

> . . . no clear reason is given why society should be stratified in the elaborate way that is described. The aim is not economic exploitation, but the desire to bully and dominate does not seem to be a motive either. There is no power-hunger, no sadism, no hardness of any kind. Those at the top have no strong motive for staying at the top, and though everyone is happy in a vacuous way, life has become so pointless that it is difficult to believe that such a society could endure.

Orwell's criticism directly opposes that which is sometimes made of *Nineteen Eighty-Four*: that a state founded solely on power for its own sake could not survive. But Orwell saw in the kind of sadism displayed by the Nazis an irresistible energy. The purposeless advances in science described in *Brave New World* provided no substitute. Science made physical power unnecessary, and the ultimate result is bound to be the dispensing with human beings altogether. This has very nearly happened in *Brave New World*. And when humanity no longer exists in the way we know it science becomes meaningless. Orwell insists that totalitarianism derived its energy from the exploitation of human beings, even though their major qualities were bludgeoned into dormancy.

Orwell's theory of the energy of power was closer to Jack London than to any of the books that paralleled his forecast of totalitarianism. London gives a violently savage picture of dictatorial methods and of mass reaction to them. (He himself may have been influenced by Frank Norris's *The Octopus,* a book more directly founded on contemporary reality than *The Iron Heel.*) Orwell says that London understood "just how the possessing class would behave once they were seriously menaced." *The Iron Heel* shows the extremes to which the passion for power could lead. Published in 1908 it was a strangely apt foretaste of what was to occur not in America but Europe. Orwell tempered such ferocity with the particular details he had learned from Koestler and others who described the process of interrogation and produced a mixture of sadism and cold logic. He did not think *The Iron Heel* an entirely good book, but he admired it because it did contain a feature missing, or mistakenly envisaged, in other books of prediction. "The book is chiefly notable for maintaining that capitalist society would not perish of its 'contradictions,' but that the possessing class would be able to form itself into a vast corporation and even evolve a sort of perverted Socialism, sacrificing many of its principles in order to preserve its superior status." Orwell does not tell us very much of Ingsoc's developments, but he clearly indicates, through Goldstein's theories, that this is how he visualized its coming to power.

But it was from his experience of contemporary London that Orwell drew the inspiration for the opening pages of *Nineteen Eighty-Four*. It was an experience that had also conditioned his writing of *Keep the Aspidistra Flying* and we can recognize a number of similar details:

> It was a bright cold day in April, and the clocks were striking thirteen. Winston Smith, his chin nuzzled into his breast in an effort to escape the vile wind, slipped quickly through the glass doors of Victory Mansions, though not quickly enough to prevent a swirl of gritty dust from entering along with him.
>
> The hallway smelt of boiled cabbage and old rag mats. At one end of it a coloured poster, too large for indoor display, had been tacked to the wall. It depicted simply an enormous face, more than a metre wide: the face of a man of about forty-five, with a heavy black moustache and ruggedly handsome features. Winston made for the stairs. It was no use trying the lift. Even at the best of times it was seldom working, and at present the electric current was off during daylight hours. It was part of the economy drive in preparation for Hate Week.

There are two streams of description in this passage—the familiar details of drabness, the dust, the smell, the out-of-order lift, and the individual words that disturb the familiarity and introduce a foreign and troubling note. The clock strikes thirteen, the building has a glass door, hardly compatible with the smell of cabbage, the poster is a meter wide. The phrase "Hate Week" removes all doubt that this is not the Britain of 1948. By the end of the paragraph there are further details that are important hints of the major themes and contrasts of the novel:

> The flat was seven flights up, and Winston, who was thirty-nine and had a varicose ulcer above his right ankle, went slowly, resting several times on the way. On each landing, opposite the lift shaft, the poster with the enormous face gazed from the wall. It was one of those pictures that are so contrived that the eyes follow you about when you move. BIG BROTHER IS WATCHING YOU, the caption beneath it ran.

We are told only two things about Winston, but we already see him as a frail and undistinguished man, completely dominated by his surroundings. Even against these relatively minor facts of life in Airstrip One—the stair, the poster, the lift—Winston has no authority. On the first page he is as powerless as on the last. The force of the poster grows from sentence to sentence. At first, apart from the size, it seems inoffensive, but its recurrence on each landing, the apparent movement of the eyes, lead to the starkness of the caption which baldly sums up the condition of life in 1984.

The remainder of the book enlarges this caption. On the final page everything else is subservient to it. But we have already been warned not to be surprised at anything that might follow. We know at once that Winston is a frail creature, robbed by the state of any vitality he might have had, brought to subjection by the stairs as much as by any direct wielding of authority. He has no chance of developing his vague and inarticulate revolt against the Thought Police and the telescreens that eliminate any kind of private life, and he understands this from the beginning. He is a part of the dreary, colorless background of which he is so conscious.

Winston's uneasiness at life in Oceania is aggravated by his nostalgia for a half-remembered past. It is a nostalgia very similar to George Bowling's, and the years immediately after the Second World War take on the coloring of those just before the First. The dim scenes and impressions in Winston's memory encourage him to indulge in an instinctive feeling that the quality of life has not always been the same, and in fact *should* not be as Ingsoc has made it. In his diary Winston feels his way towards revolt. It is a half-willed reaction against the Thought Police, against "the bombed sites where the plaster dust swirled in the air and the willow-herb straggled over the heaps of rubble" and above all against the Party's power over the past.

The basis of Ingsoc's revolution is the manipulation of language. The Thought Police, terror and torture are instruments of preserving order; Newspeak is a means of controlling the thoughts and inclinations that inspire disorder. Syme, Winston's colleague, describes the aim of Newspeak: "In the end we shall make thoughtcrime literally impossible, because there will be no words in which to express it. Every concept that can ever be needed will be expressed by exactly *one* word, with its meaning rightly defined and all its subsidiary meanings rubbed out and forgotten." The manipulation of language is essential to the manipulation of history, as Orwell became so much aware of at the time of the Spanish Civil War.

The Party that holds the key to forcing belief upon the public is in a position to force a certain interpretation of history. In the case of Ingsoc it is not an interpretation that is forced, but the complete destruction of history.

There is a further aspect of the manipulation of language that Orwell deals with in his appendix to *Nineteen Eighty-Four*, "The Principles of Newspeak." He made the point that the principle of abbreviation, which Newspeak adopts extensively, was a characteristic feature of political language in the first half of the century. He says:

> In the beginning the practice had been adopted as it were instinctively, but in Newspeak it was used with a conscious purpose. It was perceived that in thus abbreviating a name one narrowed and subtly altered its meaning, by cutting out most of the associations that would otherwise cling to it. The words *Communist International*, for instance, call up a composite picture of universal brotherhood, red flags, barricades, Karl Marx and the Paris Commune. The word *Comintern*, on the other hand, suggests merely a tightly-knit organisation and a well-defined body of doctrine. It refers to something almost as easily recognised, and as limited in purpose, as a chair or table. *Comintern* is a word that can be uttered almost without taking thought, whereas *Communist International* is a phrase over which one is obliged to linger at least momentarily. In the same way, the associations called up by a word like *Minitrue* are fewer and more controllable than those called up by *Ministry of Truth*.

Orwell reveals here not only an understanding of the way in which political language could be made to work, but the basis of the authenticity of Ingsoc's control. It is this that Winston begins to grasp as he discovers hints of a world that Ingsoc has tried to obliterate.

Winston's rebellion begins when he buys the notebook in which he keeps his diary. It comes to represent his boyhood, of which he is only half-conscious. He tries to force it back into his memory. But as in the process of writing his memories begin to clarify he realizes the impossibility of communicating from one generation to the next:

> For whom, it suddenly occurred to him to wonder, was he writing this diary? For the future, for the unborn. His mind hovered for a

moment round the doubtful date on the page, and he fetched up
with a bump against the Newspeak word *doublethink*. For the first
time the magnitude of what he had undertaken came home to him.
How could you communicate with the future? It was of its nature
impossible. Either the future would resemble the present, in which
case it would not listen to him: or it would be different from it,
and his predicament would be meaningless.

The frailty of Winston's position is underlined. He can find no
intellectual support for his instinctive revolt. Ingsoc has brought
history to a standstill, and has wiped out the relevance of such actions as writing down one's private thoughts. The only function
Winston's diary can perform is to provide the means of betrayal to
the Thought Police.

Certainty of failure is in front of him, yet Winston moves on to
the next stage in his rebellion, his affair with Julia. When he first
encounters her he takes her for what she seems, a blind, hearty wor-
shipper of Big Brother. But in fact Julia is also involved in an instinctive revolt, a revolt against the Party's control of private pleasure. "The aim of the Party was not merely to prevent men and
women from forming loyalties which it might not be able to control.
Its real, undeclared purpose was to remove all pleasure from the
sexual act. Not love so much as eroticism was the enemy . . ." For
Julia revolt entails cheating the Party of this control. She does not
seek an intellectual basis, she is not concerned with the past. Her
affair with Winston entirely satisfies her urge to revolt.

Winston shares her feelings, but his revolt is not contained by
them. For him sex represents an energy that can be both creative
and corrupting. "Who knew, perhaps the Party was rotten under
the surface, its cult of strenuousness and self-denial simply a sham
concealing iniquity. If he could have infected the whole lot of them
with leprosy or syphilis, how gladly he would have done so!" He
believes in the "animal instinct, the simple undifferentiated desire:
that was the force that would tear the Party to pieces." But just as
it is a force that could perhaps corrupt the Party from within and
also act against it from without, it can both stimulate the instinct
to rebel and deflect it. Julia does not feel the need for revolt in a
larger sphere than that of private pleasure. Winston seeks restlessly

for a means of striking a blow against the perversion of language and history.

Winston's attempt to piece together some impression of the past leads him to the district inhabited by the proles, the majority of the population kept in a condition of complete suppression as a necessary and uncomplaining labor force. To Winston the proles are a seething mass of energy which, properly directed, could break the Party's grip. He soon discovers that they are not aware of their own potential. It is a problem that Rubashov also ponders: there can be no revolution without the people's consciousness of their condition, and they cannot acquire this consciousness with revolution. Hope lies in the proles, Winston says. But the condition of the proles is hopeless.

The old, crumbling part of London works on Winston's memory. He finds a junk shop with a room above it filled with curiosities from the past. His instinctive feeling for history returns. The room "had awakened in him a sort of nostalgia, a sort of ancestral memory. It seemed to him that he knew exactly what it felt like to sit in a room like this, in an arm-chair beside an open fire with your feet on the fender and the kettle on the hob . . ." It is again the *Wigan Pier* nostalgic interior. Winston's visit to the country with Julia has a similar quality: it is much happier than the outing of Gordon and Rosemary. But the moments of warmth and comfort, or of light relief, are brief. They are just long enough to hint that life could be better. Winston's more usual surroundings are these:

> A low-ceilinged, crowded room, its walls grimy from the contact of innumerable bodies; battered metal tables and chairs, placed so close together that you sat with elbows touching; bent spoons, dented trays, coarse white mugs; all surfaces greasy, grime in every crack; a sourish composite smell of bad gin and bad coffee and metallic stew and dirty clothes. Always in your stomach and in your skin there was a sort of protest, a feeling that you had been cheated of something that you had a right to.

The disgust here outdoes that in the scenes of physical torture. This was Orwell recoiling from a scene that he himself could have experienced in many of its details. Scenes of contrast with this kind of thing occur seldom, but they have an important function. They are, of course, a stimulus to Winston's revolt, but they also provide small areas of warmth and reality that help to convince us of the genuineness of the love of Winston and Julia. The room above the junk shop with its decay and its rats becomes an interior in which they can build their own world. Compared with the outside reality it is pleasant and comfortable. They make real coffee and eat real bread with real jam. The food has a solid substance which the synthetic canteen stew has not.

Winston's contact with O'Brien is the third stage in his revolt. Julia, in spite of her philosophy of "the clever thing was to break the rules and stay alive all the same," accompanies him on his visit. O'Brien is a more difficult and puzzling character than any other Orwell created. He is physically unattractive, yet has an outgoing charm—"a large, burly man with a thick neck and a coarse, humorous, brutal face. In spite of his formidable appearance he had a certain charm of manner. He had a trick of resettling his spectacles on his nose which was curiously disarming . . ." Early in the novel the charm predominates. Winston feels that O'Brien will be sympathetic to his unease. He interprets the tiniest gesture in favor of what he wants to believe. But always he has a sense that O'Brien will destroy him, a kind of perverse knowledge that he can trust O'Brien because he will be responsible for his cure.

When O'Brien becomes Winston's torturer this duality comes into its own. O'Brien is both his destroyer and his saviour. Winston hates him for the pain which he inflicts and yet clings to him for the very reasons that he hates the Party, because he represents an absolute that is constant and unchangeable, which can remove all life's complications. Something of Winston's attitude is reflected in the way in which Orwell draws the character of O'Brien. There is both admiration and disgust in the portrayal. The duality can be explained a little by Orwell's own attitude to Hitler. Although Nazism appalled him he understood Hitler's power of attraction. "The fact is there is something deeply appealing about him. One feels it again when one sees his photographs. . . . It is a pathetic, dog-like face, the face of a man suffering under intolerable wrongs. In a rather more manly way it reproduces the expression of innumerable pictures of Christ crucified. . . . One feels, as with Napoleon, that he is fighting against destiny, that he *can't* win, and yet that he somehow deserves to. The attraction of such a pose is of course enormous; half the films that one sees turn upon some such theme." Of course, there is no suggestion that O'Brien will lose in the end, yet we do feel Orwell's admiration for him, that he half intends that O'Brien deserves to win, that it is better for Winston that O'Brien does win. O'Brien has a physical presence quite unlike Hitler's; it is more like Stalin's, but it is also like that of *The Iron Heel*'s hero Everhard. Everhard also has great physical strength—"He was a superman, a blond beast"—but he is the novel's hero and an attractive character, a man associated with "nobleness of purpose and heroism of effort." It may be that Everhard was Orwell's inspiration for O'Brien's attractive ugliness; it is a type that occurs throughout Jack London's fiction. It is not only the pathetic attraction of Hitler, but the attraction of solid physical strength, that contrasts sharply with Winston's meagreness.

Koestler's Gletkin and Nikitin are very similar, and yet we are not conscious of a duality. Nikitin's attraction, his strength and what he stands for in the Party are all one and the same thing. Gletkin seems to have physical strength because he has power. If anything we lose the sense of O'Brien's personal strength when we see him wielding instruments of torture. In exhibiting O'Brien's apparent change of character there is a change also in the quality of the characterization. His fullness of personality and presence fade as he shrinks to a mere machine for torture and justification. We never see Gletkin in any other role. O'Brien loses a dimension, yet it is important that all the elements of his personality remain, as Winston still sees him as combining charm and brutality. At the same time the transformation of O'Brien from man to machine provides an important part of the horror of the torturing scenes and ultimately of the horror of 1984. Part of Orwell's contention is that conditions could arise under which men are stripped of all personality and become emotionally and intellectually impotent. The complete picture of O'Brien is less abhorrent and more horrifying than Koestler's picture of Gletkin. Gletkin's attraction can only be intellectual. He does not have O'Brien's capacity to induce emotional faith and reliance and therefore cannot destroy such feelings.

Against the power of O'Brien we have to measure the quality of
Winston's love, for it is his relationship with Julia that is the final
test of his revolt. In his first long scene with Julia, in her country
hideout, there is an aggressive hardness about their relationship in
spite of the calmness of their surroundings. They are not able to
lose themselves in the temporary safety of their short time together.
Winston is conscious of this:

> In the old days, he thought, a man looked at a girl's body and saw
> that it was desirable, and that was the end of the story. But you
> could not have pure love and pure lust nowadays. No emotion was
> pure, because everything was mixed up with fear and hatred. Their
> embrace had been a battle, the climax a victory. It was a blow struck
> against the Party. It was a political act.

Winston realizes that he has at last acted against the Party, and
from that moment he cannot detach his love for Julia from his
revolt. They become identical. The quality of his love is contained
in the quality of his revolt, and ultimately they both prove to have
been equally inadequate.

We can never exactly distinguish between Winston's failure and
the Party's success. A stronger personality might have carried him
further; but the Party denies the possibility of such a personality,
except where it can fully utilize the strength—as in the case of
O'Brien. In the junk shop scenes the relationship of Winston and
Julia is real and intimate. They are lulled into relaxation. They
give each other's personalities a chance that they never before had.
They luxuriate in their privateness and in the sense of the past that
the room generates. Winston remembers his mother as possessing
"a kind of nobility, a kind of purity, simply because the standards
that she obeyed were private ones." Thinking themselves secure
from the Thought Police Winston and Julia make a start in the
search for standards. But the purity and nobility are beyond them:

> The terrible thing that the Party had done was to persuade you that
> mere impulses, mere feelings, were of no account, while at the same
> time robbing you of all power over the material world. When once
> you were in the grip of the Party, what you felt or did not feel,
> what you did or refrained from doing, made literally no difference.

Whatever happened you vanished, and neither you nor your actions were ever heard of again. You were lifted clean out of the stream of history. And yet to the people of only two generations ago, this would not have seemed all-important, because they were not attempting to alter history. They were governed by private loyalties which they did not question. What mattered were individual relationships, and a completely helpless gesture, an embrace, a tear, a word spoken to a dying man, could have value in itself. The proles, it suddenly occurred to him, had remained in this condition. They were not loyal to a party or a country or an idea, they were loyal to one another. . . . The proles had stayed human.

Against such odds Winston's love is nullified. It can never have value as an end in itself. The qualities that might have enabled him to resist betrayal have been extinguished from all humanity except the proles, and the proles do not know how to utilize such qualities.

Winston's perception and fear are matched against an irrational belief in himself. He believes that the Party cannot touch his inner feelings. "What you say or do doesn't matter: only feelings matter. If they could make me stop loving you—that would be the real betrayal." "If you can *feel* that staying alive is worth while, even when it can't have any result whatever, you've beaten them." Of course, they do make him stop loving Julia and kill his belief that staying alive is worth while. Even while Winston is saying this he knows that every part of himself and Julia are vulnerable to the Party. Their betrayal of each other is already inevitable.

The duality of Winston's attitude to O'Brien is complemented by the duality of his love. It is emphasized by the gulf that has always existed between himself and Julia. Julia's private rebellion is enough for her—she falls asleep while Winston is reading Goldstein aloud. He resents Julia's attitude, yet will not admit that it represents a serious difference between them. He has little more than their relationship to sustain his revolt.

He finds intellectual sustenance in the work of Goldstein, *Nineteen Eighty-Four*'s Trotsky figure. The book contains lengthy extracts from Goldstein's writings. This serves to explain a situation that for most of the novel has been more emotionally real than intellectually probable. Goldstein's theories are developments of many of the ideas that had been characteristic of Orwell's thinking for some years; they also ingeniously echo the tone and phrasing of the writings of Trotsky himself. They explain that the invincibility of Ingsoc rests on two foundations: the perversion of language and the fact of perpetual war. War on a limited scale is an ideal way of controlling the energies of the population:

> The essential act of war is destruction, not necessarily of human lives, but of the products of human labour. War is a way of shattering to pieces, or pouring into the stratosphere, or sinking in the depths of the sea, materials which might otherwise be used to make the masses too comfortable, and hence, in the long run, too intelligent. Even when weapons of war are not actually destroyed, their manufacture is still a convenient way of expending labour power without producing anything that can be consumed.

War is being used as a means of controlling the population of the State's own territory rather than of destroying or conquering enemy territory. It is a concept that Orwell frequently touched on, and, for us now, perhaps represents the most valuable warning the book contains. The connection that he draws between a totalitarian society and atomic war is still very relevant. It is worth quoting at length from an article by Erich Fromm, written in 1961, in which he explains this relevance:

> Orwell's picture is so pertinent because it offers a telling argument against the popular idea that we can save freedom and democracy by continuing the arms race and finding a "stable" deterrent. This soothing picture ignores the fact that with increasing technical "progress" (which creates entirely new weapons about every 5 years, and will soon permit the development of 100 or 1000 instead of 10 megaton bombs), the whole society will be forced to live underground, but that the destructive strength of thermonuclear bombs will always remain greater than the depth of the caves, that the military will become dominant (in fact, if not in law), that fright and hatred of a possible aggressor will destroy the basic attitudes of a democratic, humanistic society. In other words, the continued arms race, even if it would not lead to the outbreak of thermonuclear war, would lead to the destruction of any of those qualities of our society

that can be called "democratic," "free," or "in the American tradition."

Fromm goes on to say that *Nineteen Eighty-Four* "is simply implying that the new form of managerial industrialism, in which man builds machines which act like men and develops men who act like machines, is conducive to an era of dehumanization and complete alienation, in which men are transformed into things and become appendices to the process of production and consumption." Orwell's theory of Oceanic society is perhaps more feasible than its reality—and yet, of course, they cannot be separated. Fromm sharply indicates the force of the connection between a dehumanized society and perpetual war, or preparation for war. As well as the more concrete links, perpetual war can be exploited as a continual crisis which demands continual sacrifice on the part of the individual on behalf of the state. The creed of Ingsoc is not in itself sufficient to sustain the adulation of Big Brother and thereby the order of society. There needs to be a monstrous threat from outside to enable the machinery of authority to function with complete efficiency inside. And if the threat does not exist it has to be created. This situation is not merely an intellectual one. The basic elements were apparent in the heightened period of the cold war, and can be seen now in, for example, China's exploitation of American intervention in Vietnam, or the United States' similar use of the threat of Communism in Latin America.

It is clear, both from Goldstein and from Orwell's previous writings, that he was entirely conscious of the implications of the structure of Oceanic society and the division of the world, and of its basis in contemporary reality. It is this that maintains the book's relevance long after we have ceased to speculate as to what particular details of life in *Nineteen Eighty-Four* will match those in 1984.

The reading of Goldstein is, as it were, the book's theoretical climax. What follows is concerned with the arrest and torture of Winston, his betrayal of Julia and his acceptance of Big Brother. His defeat has been implied from the first pages. Orwell builds it up into a second climax of horror and disgust. Physical torture is an accepted factor in the methods of sustaining a totalitarian régime, and Orwell was clearly determined to present elaborate details, although he himself had had no experience of imprisonment or torture. It is here that we feel the strain on Orwell's imagination. Pain is used as therapy. The enforcing of the Party's perverted logic into Winston's mind is seen as a cure. O'Brien is the surgeon. Orwell tries to indicate precisely the relationship between degrees of pain and the breaking down of Winston's resistance, and in the earlier stages he is successful. The process is quite different from the interrogation of Rubashov. There are other factors involved. Winston's regard for O'Brien is not destroyed—he wants to believe that O'Brien is holding up five fingers, although he can only see four. But Winston's intellect will not accept what his emotions and imagination are eager to embrace. It is O'Brien's task to cut out the section of resistance in Winston's brain, and to replace it by an absolute faith that has nothing whatever to do with logic in the truth of what the Party states. He succeeds, and Winston actually sees five fingers:

> He saw five fingers, and there was no deformity. Then everything was normal again, and the old fear, the hatred, and the bewilderment came crowding back again. But there had been a moment—he did not know how long, thirty seconds perhaps—of luminous certainty, when each new suggestion of O'Brien's had filled up a patch of emptiness and become absolute truth, and two and two could have been three as easily as five, if that were what was needed.

Winston's relief at finding a moment of "luminous certainty" is a part of the general inclination in humanity to have life made easier by absolute faith. By this time circumstances are just too difficult for Winston to apprehend. He realizes that the only way in which life—if he is allowed to live—will be endurable is by accepting blindly everything that O'Brien suggests. He wills himself to this acceptance, but has to know first why the Party needs to have this power over him. O'Brien explains. "Power is not a means to an end. One does not establish a dictatorship in order to safeguard a revolution; one makes the revolution in order to establish the dictatorship. The object of persecution is persecution. The object of torture is torture. The object of power is power." As Winston perceived there is no question of right or wrong involved in this, no discussion of ends and means. Rubashov's dialogue is irrelevant. Even the necessity of justification has been removed. The Party has achieved its aim so effectively that the intellect is blunted and the emotions are channelled into hysteria.

O'Brien insists that Ingsoc has created a Party which has a vitality and force that is entirely independent of individuals. Human life is not its sustaining energy—it sustains human life, or destroys it, at will. O'Brien says: "You are imagining that there is something called human nature which will be outraged by what we do and will turn against us. But we create human nature." Finally, O'Brien himself is no different from Winston, except that he is more thoroughly under the Party's control.

One level of Winston's resistance remains, and at this stage he himself is only half aware of it. He slowly finds that he can quite naturally articulate the Party's slogans. He can easily dismiss the occasional doubts—"What knowledge have we of anything, save through our own minds? All happenings are in the mind. Whatever happens in all minds, truly happens." But torture has not been able to break the thread of his memory, and memory leads him back to Julia. He still loves Julia. He realizes that "It was more difficult than accepting an intellectual discipline. It was a question of degrading himself, mutilating himself. He had got to plunge into the filthiest of filth." The final stage in the torture, the final degradation, is Room 101.

In Room 101 Winston has to face being eaten alive by rats, of which he has an uncontrollable, hysterical fear. His betrayal of Julia is violent and final. "For an instant he was insane, a screaming animal. Yet he came out of the blackness clutching an idea. There was one and only one way to save himself. He must interpose another human being, the *body* of another human being between himself and the rats." The human being he calls upon is Julia. At this moment Winston relinquishes complete control of himself to the Party. He is cured. He himself denies, wipes out, his final personal loyalty and there ceases to be any hope for him as an independent human being.

The remaining pages of the book return us to the drab atmosphere of the opening. Winston has become a feeble, gin-soaked creature. He encounters Julia who has been put through the same process of rehabilitation. The only emotion they are capable of is hatred, and even that is half-hearted. But the announcement of a military victory stirs Winston to tears: he loves Big Brother.

Orwell himself was not happy about Room 101. He was searching for a climax to the devastation of human individuality, and although he does succeed in communicating the reality of the rats, he does not convince us that they represent the ultimate in horror. In a letter to Julian Symons he wrote, in answer to criticisms of this scene, "You are of course right about the vulgarity of the 'Room 101' business. I was aware of this while writing it, but didn't know another way of getting somewhere near the effect I wanted." Some kind of climax was obviously necessary. We know throughout the book that the Party will defeat Winston, and therefore the end must be something more than the mere working out of our expectations. We need to be shocked. Clearly, Orwell's own lack of experience reduced the range of detail he could communicate. It would have been too risky to rely on second-hand accounts for the final stage in the horror. Typically, perhaps, he chose to exploit a commonplace, a fear that his readers should have been able to feel much more intimately than Gestapo methods. And there is no logical reason why rats should not be so terrible as complicated machines of torture. In theory the switch from machine-made horror to natural horror should have been effective, but Room 101 does not stun quite in the way it should. Part of the failing lies in Winston's own reaction: the active side of the horror is convincing, the reactive side we suspect of being forced. Winston's response is very specific and in no particular way connected with the nature of the torture. He is neither totally irrational in his hysteria nor is his mind in control of what he says. The result is unsatisfactory. It is of course hard to assess a passage of writing conceived entirely in terms of extremes, for it is in the very nature of an extreme situation that anything is both possible and probable. But Orwell, in forcing so much to rely on this incident, is perhaps overloading with particularity a scene which would have been more successful as a general climax of horror.

An evaluation of a novel like *Nineteen Eighty-Four* must be undertaken in terms of the effect which it had, of whether the message was received as it was delivered. To this extent characterization is instrumental. On the whole we feel no particular attraction for Winston or Julia. We are interested in the nature of their revolt. However, if the instruments are flawed the purpose cannot be achieved with complete success. Many critics based a rejection of *Nineteen Eighty-Four* on a failure of characterization. Tom Hopkinson and Christopher Hollis for instance. At the same time some, notably Irving Howe, went to some length to illustrate how the nature of the society Orwell describes precisely determines the personalities dominated by it. This could be developed as a blanket excuse for any apparent flaw in the novel; it is necessary to recognize that those details which result from the picture of society also contribute to it. Winston is in many respects a more rounded and sympathetic character than most of Orwell's creations. His conflict is more genuine and less perverse than that of Gordon Comstock. He is less preoccupied with himself and with the meaning of his own personal revolt. His affair with Julia, though its foundations may be shaky, is more immediate and more intimately presented than that of Gordon and Rosemary in *Keep the Aspidistra Flying*. The difficulties Gordon has to overcome flatten his personality as it flattens his resistance. Until the final pages Winston's personality is rounded by his revolt. In his case the way in which he faces impossibility gives him depth of character, and although Julia remains rather mindless she becomes a part of this depth. The growth of Winston's consciousness is closely geared to the realities of life in a situation where an improbable vision would have been the more natural reaction. His characterization is not hampered by small obsessions. Ultimately, of course, Winston achieves far less than Gordon and becomes completely lifeless, without even Gordon's truculence. But Winston emerges favorably from a comparison with almost all Orwell's pre-war characters.

*Nineteen Eighty-Four* had an electrifying effect on the public. A first impression of over twenty-six thousand copies was printed. Compared with the fifteen hundred copies sold of *Homage to Catalonia* and *Animal Farm*'s first impression of forty-five hundred, this

marked a vast change in the anticipated public response. Reviewers
who had previously been more critical than approving acclaimed
the book. V. S. Pritchett wrote: "The faults of Orwell as a writer—
monotony, nagging, the lonely schoolboy shambling down the one
dispiriting track—are transformed now he rises to a larger subject"
and "The heart sinks but the spirit rebels as one reads Mr. Orwell's
ruthless opening page. . . ." The *Times Literary Supplement* reviewer wrote: "the last word about this book must be one of thanks,
rather than criticism: thanks for a writer who deals with the problems of the world rather than the ingrowing pains of individuals,
and who is able to speak clearly and with originality on the nature
of reality and the terrors of power." In contrast, one reviewer dismissed the book as being "stale news."

It is important to note in what light *Nineteen Eighty-Four* was
praised, for in this lies our judgment of success. In Britain it was
not, on the whole, immediately received as a blow struck for Con-
servatism. In the United States, however, many reviews, particularly
in provincial and religious newspapers, hailed the book as a weapon
to be used on behalf of the right. And it was, of course, reviled by
Communists. It is clear that Orwell did not intend *Nineteen Eighty-
Four* as a statement of his rejection of socialist principles. It would
have been entirely inconsistent with his writing career if he had
not found a more direct method of articulating any change in attitude. There is no indication in the work of the last years of his life
that the motives for writing the book were other than those already
described. Crudely put, Orwell's message had always been "keep
humanity human," and he spent his life in trying to show how
Conservative values involved a denial of the right of fulfilment to
a large section of humanity. He deplored Soviet society precisely
because of its corruption of socialist principles. On the other side,
he deplored the still remaining dictatorships of Franco and Salazar,
so often apologized for by the right in Britain. It meant little to
Orwell in what name men acted. It was the quality and the consequences of their actions that he judged.

Orwell's compulsion to present his beliefs honestly and without
compromise put him in a vulnerable position, from which he could

not extricate himself by means of good faith. The root of the book's vulnerability is described by Isaac Deutscher:

> A book like *1984* may be used without much regard for the author's intention. . . . Nor need a book like *1984* be a literary masterpiece or even an important and original work to make its impact. Indeed a work of great literary merit is usually too rich in its texture and too subtle in thought and form to lend itself to adventitious exploitation. As a rule its symbols cannot easily be transformed into hypnotising bogies, or its ideas turned into slogans. The words of a great poet when, they enter the political vocabulary do so by a process of slow, almost imperceptible infiltration, not by a frantic incursion. The literary masterpiece influences the political mind by fertilising and enriching it from the inside, not by stunning it.

It cannot be denied that *Nineteen Eighty-Four* can be dangerous, and can become something quite different from what Orwell intended, in the hands of those who wish to exploit it. But the implications of Deutscher's remarks, and they are substantiated in the remainder of his article, are more than this. He suggests that *Nineteen Eighty-Four* is an undistinguished book, that because of its immediate impact and its popularity it cannot be good in literary terms. We do not have to go far to find examples of great novels that were received immediately, made a "frantic incursion," into the public consciousness; Scott and Dickens provide many. It is a fallacy that the influence of literary greatness must necessarily be slow and subtle. The immediate does not necessarily preclude the long-lasting.

No work of literature is so subtle that it can prevent parody, and the kind of exploitation that Deutscher warns against is a species of parody. Of course language is powerful; it is also just too fragile to prevent distortion. Deutscher suggests that the symbols and ideas of Orwell's novel are superficial because they can be "transformed into hypnotising bogies" and "turned into slogans." As Orwell was writing precisely about slogans and hypnotizing bogies and their effects on ordinary human life this becomes rather a cheap point. Most of Deutscher's remarks are in general true, but not necessarily, and to array them as a list of rules against which *Nineteen Eighty-Four* must be tested is bound to be misleading.

Yet Deutscher makes an important and legitimate political point, and a political novel must be able to stand up to political criticism. He warns that it is impossible to control the way in which a book is used, and because of this, whatever Orwell's intentions, *Nineteen Eighty-Four* can be described as a weapon for the right if it is used as such. There is no doubt that it has been used as such. However strongly we point out that this is not a legitimate use of the novel, that all the evidence points to a different interpretation, Deutscher's point remains crucial. However, he states his criticism in such a way that it almost becomes possible to reverse his argument, and say that the form of the novel necessarily invites a certain flexibility of interpretation which a mere political tract does not, and therefore it is to the credit of *Nineteen Eighty-Four* that it can be variously understood. In fact, Deutscher is directing an attack against the novel as a genre used for propagandist purposes, basing it on reasons rather different from those of the literary critics. He criticizes political fiction because it is less explicit than direct political expression.

Deutscher's most significant point is the making of a distinction between different processes of influence. It is evident in the reaction to the book that its effect was indeed to stun, and that it still stuns now. Orwell had established a relationship between different elements of society and of political endeavor which no one had before perceived. But it is also clear that the shocking impact does not preclude a perfectly cogent response. The power of the book to stun lies in its power to force readers to see the connections Orwell makes. It would otherwise have as fleeting an effect as an indifferent horror film, whose influence drops away as soon as one leaves the cinema.

*Nineteen Eighty-Four* stunned its readers into perception in the same way as a man suffering from amnesia can be stunned into remembering the past. The response to the book was not dulled, although it was at times misdirected. And it is important that the book still legitimately retains its force, and is still relevant, as Erich Fromm has shown. The vocabulary it injected so precipitately into the English language also remains. Big Brother is almost as famous as Falstaff or Frankenstein. The initial impact relies on whether tension is maintained. Orwell is not so much concerned with building up suspense as with shifting without warning the levels and the quality of the intensity, and in turn blurring and clarifying the edges between hope and despair. Sometimes they are in savage conflict, as when Winston begins to keep his diary, sometimes terror seems to melt away, as when Winston and Julia go to the country. Although the frame around the characters' existence is in fact rigid, it appears to be constantly shifting.

Orwell himself admitted that *Nineteen Eighty-Four* was affected by his illness. The book might have been less artistically troubling if there had been greater scope for the shifts in tension. On the other hand, it is probable that Orwell's illness gave the book the uncompromising urgency which helped to force it into the public's mind. The exaggeration of some of the claims made for the book, on either side, is a symptom of the exaggerative quality of parts of it. But never had Orwell been so irresistible.

# Orwell Looks at the World

## by Conor Cruise O'Brien

"I knew that I had a facility with words and a power of facing unpleasant facts, and I felt that this created a sort of private world in which I could get my own back for my failure in everyday life." These words, about himself as a boy, Orwell wrote when he was already near his death; and they are both true and an example of their own truth. Not that objectively Orwell was a failure, at school or in life. But he did feel himself to be a failure; he did want to get his own back; he had the ability to face unpleasant facts and knew that ability to be, in his own carefully chosen word, "a power." In the same sentence he demonstrates his possession of that power by facing two facts about himself: his sense of failure and desire to get his own back. "I am going to tell you some facts about yourself," he says in effect to the left-wing intellectuals who were for long almost his only readers, "but first you must recognize that I face unpleasant facts about myself, and face such facts in person— facts like bullets. These are things that most of you are very little inclined to do. Through my skill with words, and the power which such skill exerts over people like you, I am now going to compel you to face at least some of the facts which you are trying to hide from yourselves and others."

Most of those addressed—perhaps on this page I can say "most of us"—responded to this challenge, I suppose, in one or both of two opposite ways. The first way was to admit that Orwell's criticisms were largely true: that left-wing intellectuals were, too often,

"Orwell Looks at the World." From *Writers and Politics,* by Conor Cruise O'Brien (London: Chatto and Windus, 1965). © 1965 by Conor Cruise O'Brien. Reprinted by permission of Pantheon Books/A Division of Random House, Inc., and Elaine Greene Ltd.

intellectually dishonest, selective in their moral indignation, furtive worshippers of power, and startlingly ignorant both of political realities and of the working class. The quantity and quality of this acceptance no doubt varied. You could, for example, accept Orwell's indictment as being true about your friends but not about yourself. Or you could, if you wanted to, drop being a leftist—for motives probably even less admirable than those which had taken you to the left—have your eyes conveniently "opened" by Orwell's fearless honesty. Some of Orwell's American admirers in the fifties may have been, in reality, more impressed by the arguments of Senator McCarthy than by those of *Animal Farm,* but an Orwellian conversion lent dignity to retreat. There were certainly also, among those clever and anxious people whom Orwell addressed, those who actually enjoyed submitting to the punishment which he inflicted:

> *Come fix upon me that accusing eye*
> *I thirst for accusation.*

But the main reason why many intellectuals accepted the truth of Orwell's accusations is that so many of these accusations were true, and the lucidity of Orwell's prose made their truth inescapable. Intellectuals are probably not more dishonest than other people; their resources for self-deception are of course much greater, but then so is their compulsion to self-criticism: greater forces committed on both sides, and the result equally uncertain. But one characteristic which the intellectual must have, or he ceases to be an intellectual at all, is the ability to see when a real point has been made in debate. It was impossible for anyone with that ability not to notice that Orwell kept scoring direct hits. You knew that certain things he said were true, because you winced when you heard them.

There can be little doubt that Orwell did change the minds of quite a few people through whom he changed the minds of many others. He cleared out a great deal of cant, self-deception, and self-righteousness, and in doing so shook the confidence of the English left, perhaps permanently. The right, as everyone knows, paid no attention to him except for the valuable ammunition he was to supply against communism, and retained its own variety of cant, almost undamaged. But the cant of the left, that cant which has so far proved indispensable to the victory of any mass movement, was almost destroyed by Orwell's attacks, which put out of action so much cant-producing machinery in its factories: the minds of left-wing intellectuals. His effect on the English left might be compared to that of Voltaire on the French nobility: he weakened their belief in their own ideology, made them ashamed of their clichés, left them intellectually more scrupulous and more defenseless.

There was, of course, and is, a second way of responding to Orwell's challenge: you could question his impartiality and therefore his right to judge. But Orwell has been accused of being essentially a reactionary writer whose work both "objectively" strengthened, and was intended to strengthen, the existing order. On this view the critique of that order which his works contain is held to be perfunctory, a sort of diversion to draw attention from the real attack, which was directed against the left. In its extreme forms, this accusation is very easy to refute. Anyone who calls Orwell a fascist—and I believe the thing has been done—knows nothing at all about either him or his life. Orwell's life, and the Spanish wound which shortened that life, refuted such absurdities. But if no human type, except perhaps the Communist party member, could be more remote from Orwell than is the fascist, it is also true that he is very far indeed from being "progressive."

Sir Richard Rees, in his sympathetic and enlightening book,[1] brings out well the "old-fashioned" side of Orwell—the deep English patriotism, the distaste for machinery and modern psychology, the love of the country, of animals, even the lingering nostalgia for the Edwardian age. These qualities, in Orwell's work, growl in many asides, and growl increasingly often. It is a Tory growl: each quality in itself, obviously, is not necessarily Tory, but grouped together they do form a Tory pattern. It is not surprising that Orwell should have taken pleasure in defending Kipling against leftist criticism (his important essay on Kipling is unaccountably omitted from the present volume[2] of collected essays, the title of which is

1 *George Orwell.*
2 *Collected Essays.*

misleading). If we add to the list a chivalrous but rather insensitive attitude towards the underdog and a tendency towards self-immolation, what seems to emerge is the character of an English conservative eccentric.

The character is on the whole an attractive one, and has done much to make English life more decent—a favorite word of Orwell's. The limitations of the viewpoint it implies are probably more obvious to foreigners than they are to the English. Orwell seldom wrote about foreigners, except sociologically, and then in a hit-or-miss fashion otherwise unusual with him; he very rarely mentions a foreign writer and has an excessive dislike of foreign words; although he condemns imperialism he dislikes its victims even more. Indeed he sometimes goes beyond dislike; he rises to something like hysteria. In *Shooting an Elephant,* he records fantasies about sticking a bayonet into the belly of a sniggering Buddhist priest. This is the kind of fantasy that Orwell himself found sinister in *No Orchids for Miss Blandish*. It is really more disquieting in *Shooting an Elephant*: not that sadistic fantasies are unusual, even in good and gentle men, but that quite unmistakably Orwell was much more likely to have this kind of fantasy about a Burmese than about an Englishman.

I do not suggest that it is morally better to have such fantasies about an Englishman. The point is that if sadistic fantasies are unevenly distributed by race or nationality, the consequences are more likely to be political—and therefore contagious and dangerous—than if they remain purely personal.

Orwell of course was too decent and clear-headed to support any racialist or imperialist program. The presence in his make-up of the kind of feeling that inspires such programs led to no more than a certain deadening of his feeling and understanding where most of the population of the world was concerned. He turned towards foreigners, especially Asians, that part of his mind which brooded darkly about sandals, beards and vegetarians. He could not "think himself into the mind" of any kind of foreigner and he seldom tried to do so. He never thought it worth while to imagine seriously what it would be like to belong to a people with a quite different historical experience from that of the English. As far as he considered such matters at all, I think he felt that not to be a product of English history was a sort of moral lapse.

Many people, quite obviously, are not less insular today than Orwell, but no one of comparable intelligence can now attain that degree of insularity—short of being whimsical like Mr. Evelyn Waugh or Mr. Kingsley Amis. During almost all of Orwell's writing career, England was sufficiently central to the world's political and economic life for an Anglocentric view of the world not to be seen as an eccentric one. Since then, the McCarthy years, the "thaw" in Russia, the rise of African nationalism, the Common Market in Europe, the ferment in Latin America, the Russian-American space race, emanations of Communist China and, in a different category, the Suez experiment and its failure have made a world in which much, though not all, of Orwell's writing must seem, to readers outside these islands, somewhat provincial.

We are near enough now to 1984 to see that the world then, whatever it may be like, will not be very like Orwell's imagining of it. Is it fantastic to see in Orwell's *1984* the reflection of a feeling that a world in which the pre-1914 British way of life had totally passed away must necessarily be a dehumanized world? And is it altogether wrong to see the inhabitants of *Animal Farm* as having points in common, not merely with Soviet Russians, but also with Kipling's lesser breeds generally, as well as with Flory's Burmese who, once the relative decencies of the Raj are gone, must inevitably fall under the obscene domination of their own kind?

To insist on the limitations of Orwell's thought is only to establish the limits within which we admire him. How much there is to admire, how much we owe to him, every page in these collected essays reminds us. That spare, tough prose has not aged; that clear eye sees more than ours do even if there are things which it cannot see through, and which we now can see from the other side in time. What political writer now cares as much as he did, both about what he is writing and about how he is writing it? Subsequent writers who exploited anger seem far off and apathetic compared with this careful writer who tried so hard to keep his judgment and his language from being clouded by an anger as real as Swift's.

# Prose Like a Window-Pane

## by George Woodcock

"What is above all needed is to let the meaning choose the word." This phrase, which provides the keynote to Orwell's recommendations for the regeneration of the English language, might also be taken to summarize the attitude towards literary form which he developed during the part of his writing life that is known to us. The thought he had to express always came first into his mind, and the form was selected, in so far as an artist ever does select deliberately, to present with the greatest effectiveness the message he wished to convey. In "Why I Write" he explains:

> My starting point is always a feeling of partisanship, a sense of injustice. When I sit down to write a book, I do not say to myself, "I am going to produce a work of art." I write because there is some lie that I want to expose, some fact to which I want to draw attention, and my initial concern is to get a hearing.

At the same time form and style were, for him, no mere mechanisms for the achievement of clear expression. One need only compare *The Road to Wigan Pier* with reports on slum conditions prepared by trained sociologists to realize that what Orwell has produced is something very different from ordinary competent expository writing. In the selection of words, in the shape of sentences, in the arrangement of incident and argument, there is an individual sensibility at work, a mind that operates by other rules than those of mere utility. As Orwell himself remarked, he could not write even in an expository sense if he did not find it also an aesthetic experience.

"Prose Like a Window-Pane." From *The Crystal Spirit,* by George Woodcock (London: Jonathan Cape Ltd., 1967), pp. 263–79. Reprinted by permission of Jonathan Cape Ltd., and Little, Brown and Company.

Nevertheless, Orwell's "partisanship" significantly affected the nature of his approach to the art of writing. Always he wrote to a purpose outside writing itself, so that the form of the work of literature was never, for him, an end in itself, and he never indulged in stylistic experimentation for its own sake. Even in discussing other writers, he soon tired of the formal aspects of their work, no matter how deliberately and effectively these may have been cultivated. His essay on Yeats, for example, begins with a singularly feeble attempt at verbal analysis, noting an affected use of the word "that" ("Or that William Blake"), remarking that certain phrases "suddenly overwhelm one like a girl's face across a room," commenting that Yeats "does not flinch from a squashy vulgar word like 'loveliness,'" and showing the lack of seriousness with which he approaches such analysis by lazily confessing that he is merely quoting from memory. But as soon as he begins to chew on what for him is the meat of the subject, the ideas and the moral impulses that underlie Yeats's poems, his essay suddenly takes on pace and authority, and the schoolboyish ineptitude of the opening stylistic discussion completely vanishes.

If we can accept what Orwell tells us in "Why I Write" about his literary development it seems evident that the extra-artistic impulse was always the starting-point of his writing. As a child, he tells us, he began to make up stories and to write poems because he recognized within him "a facility with words and a power of facing unpleasant facts" that enabled him to compensate for a feeling of "being isolated and undervalued." As we have seen elsewhere, Orwell is inclined to impute to himself at a very early age (he is now talking of the time when he was less than five) the kind of self-analyzing propensity which seems improbably adult for even the most precocious child. We must reserve judgment on this information, and pass to the period of Orwell's later schooldays and early manhood, on which his statements are likely to be more objectively reliable.

This is what he describes as his "non-literary" period, extending —he tells us—up to about the age of twenty-five, but clearly it was the time when the characteristic features of his attitude as a writer were first established. He did in fact carry on a certain amount of subliterary activity on a rather trivial level; he edited school magazines ("the most pitiful burlesque stuff"), and produced "made-to-order" poetry and semi-comic *vers d'occasion* "quickly, easily and without much pleasure to myself." When we remember the atrocious quality of most of the poetry which Orwell wrote and even published during the early 1930s, we can accept the implication that this early work was intrinsically valueless. More interesting is the pattern it seems to prefigure, since Orwell remained always an occasional writer. With the exception of his two worst novels, *A Clergyman's Daughter* and *Keep the Aspidistra Flying,* he appears to have produced hardly anything out of the mere decision to write a book. In almost every other case there was an "occasion," a particularly interesting experience, or an argument or fear nagging in his mind, that gave him the first impulse to write.

But the fact that writing was Orwell's special way of reacting to experience, and that he felt impelled to give his argument—no matter how much preliminary conversation there had been—a final shape in prose, is something that still has to be explained. And here he tells us that from early childhood down to his days of inner solitude in Burma he had carried on a habit of creating unspoken and unwritten literature, first by inventing crude adventure stories of which he was the hero, and afterwards by keeping running a mental narrative of "what I was doing and the things I saw." "Although I had to search, and did search, for the right words, I seemed to be making this descriptive effort almost against my will, under a kind of compulsion from outside."

The feeling of being compelled, of writing against one's will, is a common one among writers; indeed, it seems to be an essential aspect of any creative activity that much is given and motivated by some source outside reason, and the activity of the artist consists largely in shaping and controlling this element consciously and rationally. This "outside" or unconscious element remained strong in Orwell's work. The frequent emphasis in his novels on such phenomena as involuntary memory (*Coming Up for Air*), amnesia and slow recovery of memory (*A Clergyman's Daughter*), and dreams and nightmares (*Nineteen Eighty-Four*) suggests that Orwell was very much aware of the importance of extra-rational elements in human life and—equally—in literary creation.

His other important emphases are on the search for the right word, and on description. Orwell remembers himself as first selecting words for special purposes, but he tells us that later, in reading *Paradise Lost,* he all at once "discovered the joy of mere words, i.e. the sounds and associations of words." "As for the need to describe things," he adds in the same paragraph, "I knew all about it already." And he goes on to show how the double preoccupation with description and words determined the kind of books he wished to write in his youth.

> I wanted to write enormous naturalistic novels with unhappy endings, full of detailed descriptions and arresting smiles, and also full of purple passages in which words were used partly for the sake of their sound. And in fact my first completed novel, *Burmese Days,* which I wrote when I was thirty, but projected much earlier, is rather that kind of book.

Description—the urge to recount experiences, to picture scenes, to weave the odd observed facts of existence into the tapestry of prose—this is the original external purpose, to which is added very soon (at least as early as "A Hanging" and doubtless before) the desire to discuss what has been described, so that argument follows experience. The eventual narrowing of discussion into moral-political polemics is merely a further development along the same lines. But all the time there is the concern for words, in their dual role as evocative sounds and as the means to exact description and argument.

This double movement of Orwellian prose can be seen most effectively in the kind of autobiographical-polemical reportage which he developed as his most characteristic form of writing. The structure of such works is determined by the peculiar Orwellian dialectic of presenting experience and then arguing from it. It is, essentially, a logical rather than an organic structure, governed by a rather simple system of balancing members.

In each case Orwell catches our attention by a fine descriptive set piece which serves as a kind of overture. We enter *Down and Out in Paris and London* to the sound of the morning squabbles in the Rue du Coq d'Or, we slide into the world of slums and unemployment in *The Road to Wigan Pier* through the sensationally seedy entrance hall of the Bookers' lodging-house, and the whole heroic tone of *Homage to Catalonia* is set by the high-keyed moment of Orwell's meeting with the Italian militiaman in Barcelona on the eve of his own joining up to fight for the Republican cause.

The alternation of narration and argument that follows can be observed in *Down and Out in Paris and London*. The first nine chapters tell how Orwell came to be destitute in Paris, and recount his attempts to fight off starvation up to the moment when he and his friend Boris get work in the Hotel X. This section has the progressive episodic flavor of a *picaresque,* but once the heroes have found work the pace slows, the atmosphere changes, and we settle down to another nine chapters which describe, with illustrative incidents embedded in the narration, the life of a great hotel as seen from below stairs. A further three chapters supplement this description with a scullion's-eye view of a fashionable Paris restaurant, and then the whole tale of Orwell's experience of Gallic destitution is rounded off with a chapter discussing the reasons for the survival of the occupation of dish-washer. Now, in the briefest of interludes, Orwell crosses the Channel, and the balancing second part of the book begins; it is about half the length of the first part and so avoids excessive symmetry. Some ten chapters, in which narratives of wandering from spike to spike are interspersed with descriptions of tramp habits, tramp ways of earning a living, tramp jargon and so on, are devoted to the world of London down-and-outs. The final three chapters offer Orwell's general reflections on tramps and what should be done to mitigate the social problem which they represent.

Basically the same form is followed in both *The Road to Wigan Pier* and *Homage to Catalonia*. *The Road to Wigan Pier* begins with the Bookers' house, goes on to tell of Orwell's impressions in the mines and his experiences collecting information about life on the dole and slum housing, and ends with his arguments on what might be done to make conditions better. The second part (in this case the book is formally divided into two) begins with an autobiographical passage telling of Orwell's class-ridden childhood, his years in Burma and his first plunges into the underworld, as a prelude to a discussion on socialism from his own peculiar class point of view. In *Homage to Catalonia* there is again a sharp division about the middle of the book between the first part, narrating Orwell's experiences on the Aragon Front (with a central chapter of argument on the political nature of the war embedded in the narration) and the second part, which describes his return to Barcelona, the May fighting, and the proscription of POUM. As in the first section there is a central chapter on the political implications of the situation and on the dishonesty of Communist propagandists and left-wing newspaper reporters, with remoter implications in terms of the falsification of history.

It is, in each case, a simple and unsophisticated form of construction. If it is not exactly linear, one might describe it as no more than undulant. It is true that a kind of development, through experience to understanding, takes place in each book, but it is interesting to observe that while Orwell is always anxious, like the good journalist he was, to provide an opening that will immediately involve the reader, he is so little concerned about his endings that more often than not he goes out with an anticlimax. The last chapter of *Down and Out*, with its vapid good intentions, is pointlessly pathetic, while *The Road to Wigan Pier* ends in a stale joke about the middle class—"For, after all, we have nothing to lose but our aitches." Only in *Homage to Catalonia* is there a lift in tension towards the end, when Orwell and his wife flee across the frontier from Barcelona to France, and then, with considerable artistry, there is the quiet release as the travellers cross to the dreaming land of England.

Such relaxed, undeliberate forms are appropriate to books of this nature, where the material of real life needs only the minimum of arrangement—a matter of what to leave out more than anything else—and where the sheer quality of the prose can be relied on to carry the subject-matter and the argument. This is why Orwell, with his zest for description and his passion for words that give the right feeling to a scene or a thought, is probably the best writer of reportage in a whole generation.

But fiction is quite another matter, and here Orwell has tended to succeed—where he has done so—in spite of great weaknesses in characterization and structure. Several of his critics, Tom Hopkinson and Edward M. Thomas among them, have argued that Orwell only took to novels because that happened to be the genre in which everyone was writing in the 1930s. His own accounts, however, suggest that he had been ambitious to succeed in fiction since childhood, and that his failure to meet his own expectations of what a novelist should be was a matter of great disappointment to him.

His difficulties began with characterization, for, though he could admirably sketch a person he had met in real life and observed from the outside (for example, Bozo the screever in *Down and Out in Paris and London*), he found it hard to create a fictional character, observed from within, who was not filled with Orwellian attitudes, even to the point of breaking at times into his creator's language and expressing his most characteristic thoughts. One hero alone, George Bowling in *Coming Up for Air,* develops enough vital autonomy to live in our minds as a credible character, though even he has his improbabilities—can one really imagine so genially vulgar a man being as well-read, articulate and sensitive to natural beauty as Orwell suggests? In their own agonized way, Orwell's major characters do learn about existence, and so there is always some kind of development centered round them, though usually their education consists of little more than becoming sadder and wiser as they realize that for all their efforts they are merely back where they started, with their comforting illusions removed by the surgery of experience.

Orwell's characters are, in fact, singularly passive for the creations of so active a man; all the important things in their lives happen to them, and whenever they themselves try to take action, which is usually in the form of rebellion against their passive role, it ends always in futility. What he is really saying is that in life most actions and most rebellions end in rather unheroic failure, but that, at the same time, it is better to act and to rebel than to do nothing at all; the little flame of dissent, like the little bit of coral in Winston's paperweight, is what really counts.

As with Dickens it is usually Orwell's minor characters, in whom there is no pretense of either growth or inner tension, who are the most effective in their obsessive intensities—characters like Mrs. Creevy, proprietress of the evil Ringwood Academy; Ellis in *Burmese Days,* the fanatical hater of anyone with a colored skin; and even, in a way, George Bowling, who is really a comic minor character magnified, seen from the inside, and provided with a history like the tail of a comet.

If Orwell finds it hard to create thoroughly convincing major characters, it is not merely because of their passivity, or because of the flavor of ineffectuality which lingers in one's mind when the book is read and they recede in one's mental vision. It is also because they are never really defined in their relationships with other people. Gordon Comstock in *Keep the Aspidistra Flying* has three major personal relationships, with his sister, with his friend Ravelston, and with his girl Rosemary. But in no case does the relationship come alive, and this is not merely because of Gordon's phenomenal self-centeredness. It is rather because there is no real individuality about the other characters, and consequently nothing that can strike out against his egotism. The sister is a whining masochistic spinster, on whom Gordon preys constantly. We are told that he "adores" Ravelston, but in fact he makes that insipid highbrow the butt of his most vicious attacks on the intellectual establishment and on the rich, whom he hates because of his own voluntary assumption of poverty. Neither the sister nor Ravelston reacts in any meaningful way; all they show is their ineffectual willingness to be exploited and insulted indefinitely. As for Rosemary, it is true that she plays the part of the seductive and eventually rapacious siren, but it is difficult, when one reads the juvenile dialogue that goes on between her and Gordon and when one sniffs the smell of hockey-field heartiness that hangs over her, to imagine how she succeeds. *Keep the Aspidistra Flying* is, admittedly, the worst example of Orwell's failure to involve his characters in credible relationships, and this is possibly because, in creating Comstock, he concentrated so immoderately on the isolating emotion of self-pity.

In his other novels, it is where a touch of comedy or incongruity strikes a spark that his characters really come to life. Dorothy Hare's friendship with Mr. Warburton, with its ever-to-be-repelled attempts at seduction and its slight flavor of vestry daring, is the best thing in *A Clergyman's Daughter,* and infinitely more credible than the lugubrious travesties of love affairs that go on between Gordon and Rosemary, and Winston and Julia. The only marriage in Orwell's novels that really arouses one's interest is that of George and Hilda Bowling, which, by the time we come upon it, has taken on the conventions of wedded life in one of Donald McGill's postcards, with the husband perpetually suffering for the suspicions aroused by his past adventures. In *Burmese Days* there is one very convincing and moving relationship—that between Flory and Dr. Veraswami, with all its laughable misunderstandings and with the pathetic loyalty, all on one side, that rounds it off.

But *Burmese Days* contains another relationship—or perhaps rather a confrontation—which has an important bearing upon the partial nature of Orwell's success as a fiction writer. *Burmese Days* is the most conventional of Orwell's novels, and as a novel the most successful. In his other novels Orwell funnels the intensity of feeling through a single character because only one character is seen from within. But the *true* novel, as he in the end argues in his essay on Gissing, always contains "at least two characters, probably more, who are described from the inside and on the same level of probability," and *Burmese Days* is the only one among his books that meets this requirement. Both Flory and Elizabeth Lackersteen are seen from the inside. It is true that no kind of intimacy is ever established between them, but that is part of the author's intent. What does take place is a confrontation in which they act upon and help to define each other, even though, by reason of Flory's inveterate romanticism and Elizabeth's abysmal selfishness, they are always at cross purposes and never even begin to understand each other. It is a relationship in the realistic tradition, and falls into the same class as that between Pierre Bezoukhov and Hélène, or Charles and Emma Bovary.

Orwell's failures in characterization are closely connected with the failures of general structure in his books. His concentration on the word as the vital unit of literature made him neglect the larger elements of literary planning, so that—except in *Burmese Days*—

he never worked out an even approximately satisfactory form for a
larger work of fiction. It is true that he was always searching, for
the six works of fiction which he did write represented almost as
many different types. *Burmese Days* can be accepted as a true novel
in the tradition deriving from Flaubert. But it was followed by a
regression, in *A Clergyman's Daughter,* to a loose *picaresque* with
the elementary structure of a number of episodes strung on the
thread of a journey, including at least one deliberately unrealistic
passage (the Joycean scene among the derelicts in Trafalgar
Square); several of the episodes owed their presence to the author's
desire to describe his own experiences as a hop-picker, a down-and-
out in London and a teacher in a small private school rather than
to any evident needs of the plot. *Keep the Aspidistra Flying* is certainly not a novel in the traditional sense, and can probably be
most kindly described as a burlesque. *Coming Up for Air* is a kind
of prose dramatic monologue, held together mainly by the fascina-
tion of George Bowling's memories; it is a book almost without
construction, with a vast middle section devoted to the past as Bowling's mind portrays it, and a disproportionately small final section
describing episodically the trip back to Lower Binfield which is the
main action of the book. *Animal Farm,* which Orwell described as
a fairy tale, is really a fable, and it is also the only one of his books
which is engineered with perfect tightness and economy, largely
because it was built round an actual historical incident, the Russian
Revolution and its betrayal. The problems of character are mag-
nificently evaded by the stylization which becomes possible through
the substitution of animals for human beings, and the simplified
personalities that result are nearer to Jonsonian humors than to
characters in the modern sense of the word.

Finally, *Nineteen Eighty-Four* is a Utopia, even if it is seen in
negative, and, like other works of its kind, it has to find room for a
great deal of detail of a kind that would be unnecessary in an ordinary novel. Here again, though perhaps not so successfully as in
*Animal Farm,* Orwell takes a great deal more care over construction than he did in any of his pre-war books except *Burmese Days.*
He solves one of the recurrent problems of Utopian writing, that
of having to deal with the mass of unfamiliar inventions, appli-

ances and arrangements in a society of the future, by assuming that
the physical setting of London will not have changed except to the
extent of having become a great deal more decrepit; in other words,
that Utopia may be something quite different from a steel-and-con-
crete paradise—may in fact be more than anything else a state of
mind. He brings in a few inventions that are of use merely to the
police so as to show the direction society has taken, and the space
saved in this way he uses for long passages of theoretical material
relating to the new society—particularly discussions on Newspeak,
extracts from the spurious Goldstein book describing the history of
Oceania and the Party, and dialogues between Winston Smith and
O'Brien in the torture chambers. Here, of course, Orwell is adapt-
ing to fiction the pattern of his books of reportage; but while the
arrangement helps the reader to understand the didactic message
of the book, it tends to overwhelm the human drama that is—at
least in fictional terms—the heart of the book. The main flaw of
*Nineteen Eighty-Four* is in fact that it has two centers, a political
and theoretical one and a human one; these centers come together
when Winston is confronted by O'Brien in the Ministry of Love.
For this is not only the point where Winston meets the power of
the Party in all its inhumane force; it is also the point where the
essentially human contact he thought he had established with
O'Brien is betrayed. But instead of allowing the situation to speak
in these terms, Orwell entirely spoils the effect by allowing O'Brien
to argue and discourse at length, like an inverted image of himself, on the dialectics of power. Thus he fails at the crucial point to
fuse the dual purposes of the book.

Orwell established his own manner of life, his own moral-
political stance, his own way of using words, even his own form of
reportage, but he never established, at least in the larger structural
sense, a characteristic form for his fiction. Nor can it really be said
that he spent the time in experimentation, since every one of the
six different forms he took for his novels (to use the word *novel* in
its broadest sense) was a ready-made picked from the general rack
of serviceable forms developed over the centuries. It seems that just
as Orwell was not interested in creating a system for his thought,
so he was not interested in creating an overall structure within

which to write. He was content to accept the structures other men
had already developed, and even these he did not always use with
great care. Sometimes one has the impression—it happens with a
good book like *Coming Up for Air* as well as an indifferent book
like *A Clergyman's Daughter*—that he got an idea and a vague
shape in his mind and let the writing follow its course. Without
very much exaggeration one might apply to him one of his own
remarks about Dickens—"a writer whose parts are greater than
his wholes . . . all fragments, all details—rotten architecture, but
wonderful gargoyles."

But though Orwell had little sense of fictional architecture and
was a poor hand at characterization, the question as to whether he
is a writer worth reading half a generation after his death hardly
arises. He so obviously is, because what he liked doing he did su-
perlatively well. His descriptions are magnificent; his polemical
arguments, even when they occur in the wrong places, are always
intensely readable; every one of his books contains episodes which
most writers would give years of their lives to have written; his
style in the narrower sense, his way with words, is inimitable.

Not since Swift, his great master, has there been a prose more
lucid, flexible, exact and eloquent than Orwell's. But Orwell goes
beyond Swift, for he can speak in the tone of humor as well as that
of satire; he can sound the lyrical and the elegiac as well as the
urbane and austere notes, and his style is capable of many varia-
tions. The tone in which he writes of Wigan, for example, is quite
different from the tone in which he writes of Aragon, less heroic
and rhetorical, as is appropriate to the different worlds he is presenting, and the style in which he argues is different from that in
which he describes. In his fiction, even, there are several perceptibly
different forms of the Orwellian style. Here are three samples
drawn from books spaced out in terms of publication over the
twelve years from 1933 to 1945.

> In a moment the girl began to dance. But at first it was not a dance,
> it was a rhythmic nodding, posturing and twisting of the elbows,
> like the movements of one of those jointed wooden figures on an
> old-fashioned roundabout. The way her neck and elbows rotated was

precisely like a jointed doll, and yet incredibly sinuous. Her hands, twisting like snakeheads with the fingers close together, could lie back until they were almost along her forearms. By degrees her movements quickened. She began to leap from side to side, flinging herself down in a kind of curtsy and springing up again with extraordinary agility, in spite of the long *longyi* that imprisoned her feet. Then she danced in a grotesque posture as though sitting down, knees bent, body leaned forward, with her arms extended and writhing, her head also moving to the beat of the drums. The music quickened to a climax. The girl rose upright and whirled round as swiftly as a top, the panniers of her *ingyi* flying out about her like the petals of a snowdrop.     [*Burmese Days*]

The float dived straight down, I could still see it under the water, kind of dim red, and I felt the rod tighten in my hand. Christ, that feeling! The line jerking and straining and a fish on the other end of it! The others saw my rod bending, and the next moment they'd all flung their rods down and rushed round to me. I gave a terrific haul and the fish—a great huge silvery fish—came flying up through the air. The same moment all of us gave a yell of agony. The fish had slipped off the hook and fallen into shallow water where he couldn't turn over, and for perhaps a second he lay there on his side helpless. Joe flung himself down into the water, splashing us all over, and grabbed him in both hands. "I got 'im!" he yelled. The next moment he'd flung the fish on to the grass and we were all kneeling round it. How we gloated! The poor dying brute flapped up and down and his scales glistened all the colours of the rainbow. It was a huge carp, seven inches long at least, and must have weighed a quarter of a pound. How we shouted to see him!     [*Coming Up for Air*]

The windmill presented unexpected difficulties. There was a good quarry of limestone on the farm, and plenty of sand and cement had been found in one of the out-houses, so that all the materials for building were at hand. But the problem the animals could not at first solve was how to break up the stone into pieces of suitable size. There seemed no way of doing this except with picks and crowbars, which no animal could use, because no animal could stand on his hind legs. Only after weeks of vain effort did the right idea occur to somebody—namely, to utilize the force of gravity. Huge boulders,

far too big to be used as they were, were lying all over the bed of the
quarry. The animals lashed ropes round these, and then all together,
cows, horses, sheep, any animal that could lay hold of the rope—
even the pigs sometimes joined in at critical moments—they dragged
them with desperate slowness up the slope to the top of the quarry,
where they were toppled over the edge, to shatter in pieces below.
Transporting the stone when it was once broken was comparatively
simple. The horses carried it off in cartloads, the sheep dragged
single blocks, even Muriel and Benjamin yoked themselves into an
old governess-cart and did their share. By late summer a sufficient
store of stone had accumulated, and then the building began, under
the superintendence of the pigs.      [*Animal Farm*]

The first is Orwell's earliest style, somewhat ornate, but by no
means inappropriate to its rather exotic subject, a dance so stylized
that it requires a stylized description. The sentence builds up in a
series of phrases which suggest the dance's continuous movement.
There are no less than four similes in this relatively short passage,
none of them really redundant. The first, with its image of jointed
figures on an old roundabout, sets the outlandish quality of the
scene. The last gains its effect from the mild shock of thinking of
snowdrops in the steamy heat of Burma. The choice in words is
rather more pretentious and conventional in a literary way than
Orwell would later have made, and there are a number of over-
used phrases of the type he later condemned: "incredibly sinuous,"
"extraordinary agility," and so on.

The second passage shows an immense gain in vigor and immediacy. The language and the rhythms are, of course, far more collo-
quial, and the number of Latinized words is reduced to a minimum.
The sentences are short, often exclamatory, so that the excitement
builds up in a staccato rhythm quite different from the slow, fluent
rhythm of the description of the Burmese dancers. The use of metaphor is not abandoned, but it is adapted to the manner of speech,
so that all the similes are those which an ordinary man like Bowling
with a country upbringing might have used, and which, in their
proper context, retain a considerable freshness. There is a touch of
exaggeration about the phraseology, but this reflects the personality

and the humor of the speaker. It is the language of speech, using its rhythms, while the earlier language is the language of literature. One can imagine Bowling saying these words in one's ear; they project an image of the speaker as well as of the scene. One cannot imagine anyone making an oral description of the Burmese dance in language resembling that which Orwell used when he wrote *Burmese Days*.

The final extract shows the ultimate honing down of the language to a serviceable simplicity resembling that of Defoe. There is a quite deliberate formality, rather like that of an old-fashioned travel book, conveyed in the use of phrases like "namely, to utilize the force of gravity," "a sufficient store of stone," "under the superintendence of the pigs"; this is designed to establish the distance of the world of animals from that of humanity, and so paradoxically to enable us to look at humanity from the outside. But the functional quality is developed in the simplicity of the sentence-construction, in the economy of description, which tells one everything that is needed, but includes not a single unnecessary detail, and above all in the complete absence of metaphor (unless of course one might contend that the whole fable is a kind of extended metaphor). It is a model of direct, clear description, so transparent that even without the help of figures of speech we are able actually to visualize the animals at work on their human tasks.

This is the ultimate point of Orwellian simplification. But the language of *Animal Farm* is Orwell's highest literary achievement precisely because it is appropriate to that particular story. It would not be appropriate to any other, and Orwell, even at the period when he wrote it, used variant styles for other purposes. More than any other writer of his time, perhaps more than any other writer of English, he learned to "let the meaning choose the word," which meant to let every meaning choose its word and the tone of its word. The ultimate point in such a search comes when language and meaning are so close that one cannot drive the blade of a metaphorical knife between them. The style grows so near to the subject that one no longer thinks of it as a style. This Orwell succeeded in achieving more often than most other writers.

But the style, it is said rightly, is the man. And in that crystalline prose which Orwell developed so that reality could always show through its transparency, lies perhaps the greatest and certainly the most durable achievement of a good and angry man who sought for the truth because he knew that only in its air would freedom and justice survive.

# Chronology of Important Dates

| | |
|---|---|
| 25 June 1903 | Born in Motihari, Bengal, son of an agent in the Opium Department of Indian Civil Service. |
| 1907–21 | Schooling in England: Anglican convent school, St Cyprian's Preparatory School, Eton College. |
| 1922 | Joins Indian Imperial Police in Burma; serves until resignation in 1927. |
| 1928–29 | Lives mainly in Paris; publishes articles and translations. |
| 1930–32 | Lives mainly in England; publishes articles and essays; occasional teaching and tutoring. |
| 1933 | Publishes *Down and Out in Paris and London*. |
| 1934 | Publishes *Burmese Days* in New York, having failed to find an English publisher. |
| 1935 | Publishes *A Clergyman's Daughter*. |
| 1936 | Publishes *Keep the Aspidistra Flying*; travels in northern England to collect material for *The Road to Wigan Pier*; marries Eileen O'Shaughnessy 9 June; leaves for Spain and enlists in P.O.U.M. militia in December. |
| 1937 | Fighting in Spain; wounded 20 May; leaves Spain 23 June. *The Road to Wigan Pier* published 8 March. |
| 1938 | Publishes *Homage to Catalonia*. Tubercular illness: several months in sanatorium followed by visit to Morocco. |
| 1939 | Publishes *Coming Up for Air*. |
| 1940 | Publishes *Inside the Whale*. Medically unfit for army service, joins Home Guard. |

1941            Joins British Broadcasting Corporation as talks producer in
                Indian section of overseas service.

1942–43         Journalism, Home Guard, and BBC duties; resigns from
                Home Guard 23 November 1943, from BBC 24 November
                1943; becomes literary editor of Labor weekly *Tribune*; be-
                gins writing *Animal Farm*.

1945            European correspondent for *Observer*; his wife Eileen dies
                during operation 29 March; *Animal Farm* published in
                August; begins writing *Nineteen Eighty-Four*.

1946            Publishes *Critical Essays*; rents house on island of Jura.

1947            Further attacks of tuberculosis; finishes first draft of *Nine-
                teen Eighty-Four*.

1948            Continued illness; finishes second draft of *Nineteen Eighty-
                Four*.

1949            In sanatorium and hospital; marries Sonia Brownell 13 Oc-
                tober. *Nineteen Eighty-Four* published in June.

21 January      Dies of pulmonary tuberculosis.
1950

# Notes on the Editor and Contributors

RAYMOND WILLIAMS, the editor of this volume in the Twentieth Century Views series, is the author of *Culture and Society, Border Country, The Long Revolution,* and *The Country and the City.* Fellow of Jesus College, Cambridge.

TERRY EAGLETON, author of *Shakespeare and Society* and *Exiles and Emigrés,* and former editor of *Slant.* Fellow of Wadham College, Oxford.

RICHARD HOGGART, author of *The Uses of Literacy* and *Speaking to Each Other;* founder of Centre for Contemporary Cultural Studies, University of Birmingham; now with UNESCO.

LIONEL TRILLING, author of *The Liberal Imagination, The Opposing Self, Beyond Culture,* and *Sincerity and Authenticity.*

E. P. THOMPSON, author of *William Morris, Romantic to Revolutionary* and *The Making of the English Working Class.*

JOHN WAIN, author of *Hurry on Down, Living in the Present,* and other novels; Professor of Poetry, Oxford University.

STEPHEN J. GREENBLATT, author of *Three Modern Satirists* and *Sir Walter Raleigh;* Assistant Professor of English, University of California, Berkeley.

ISAAC DEUTSCHER, author of *Stalin* and a three-volume biography of Trotsky.

JENNI CALDER (nee DAICHES) author of *Chronicles of Conscience.*

CONOR CRUISE O'BRIEN, author of *Maria Cross, To Katanga and Back,* and *The Suspecting Glance;* United Nations representative in Katanga, 1961.

GEORGE WOODCOCK, author of *The Crystal Spirit;* former editor of *Now.*

# Selected Bibliography

## Books by George Orwell

*Down and Out in Paris and London.* London: Gollancz, 1933.

*Burmese Days.* New York: Harper, 1934.

*A Clergyman's Daughter.* London: Gollancz, 1935.

*Keep the Aspidistra Flying.* London: Gollancz, 1936.

*The Road to Wigan Pier.* London: Gollancz, 1937.

*Homage to Catalonia.* London: Secker & Warburg, 1938.

*Coming Up for Air.* London: Gollancz, 1939.

*Inside the Whale.* London: Gollancz, 1940.

*Animal Farm.* London: Secker & Warburg, 1945.

*Nineteen Eighty-Four.* London: Secker & Warburg, 1949.

*The Collected Essays, Journalism and Letters of George Orwell.* 4 vols., ed. Sonia Orwell and Ian Angus. London: Secker & Warburg, 1968.

## Books and Articles about Orwell

Alldritt, K. *The Making of George Orwell.* London: Edward Arnold, 1969.

Atkins, J. *George Orwell.* London: Calder, 1954.

Brander, L. *George Orwell.* London: Longmans, 1954.

Calder, J. *Chronicles of Conscience.* London: Secker & Warburg, 1968.

Cook, R. "Kipling and Orwell," *Modern Fiction Studies,* VII (Summer 1961).

Deutscher, I. *Heretics and Renegades.* London: Hamish Hamilton, 1955.

Eagleton, T. *Exiles and Emigrés.* London: Chatto & Windus, 1970.

Greenblatt, S. J. *Three Modern Satirists.* New Haven: Yale University Press, 1965.

Gross, M., ed. *The World of George Orwell*. London: Weidenfeld and Nicolson, 1971.

Heppenstall, R. *Four Absentees*. London: Barrie & Rockcliff, 1960.

Hollis, C. *A Study of George Orwell*. London: Hollis & Carter, 1956.

Hopkinson, T. *George Orwell*. London: Longmans, 1953.

Howe, I. *Politics and the Novel*. New York, 1957.

Kubal, D. L. *Outside the Whale*. Notre Dame, Ind.: University of Notre Dame Press, 1972.

Lee, R. A. *Orwell's Fiction*. Notre Dame, Ind.: University of Notre Dame Press, 1969.

Lief, R. A. *Homage to Oceania*. Columbus, Ohio: Ohio State University Press, 1969.

Oxley, B. *George Orwell*. London: Evans Brothers, 1967.

Rees, R. *George Orwell: Fugitive from the Camp of Victory*. London: Secker & Warburg, 1961.

Stansky, P. and W. Abrahams. *The Unknown Orwell*. New York: Knopf, 1972.

Thomas, E. M. *Orwell*. Edinburgh and London: Oliver & Boyd, 1965.

Vorhees, R. J. *The Paradox of George Orwell*. West Lafayette, Ind.: Purdue University Studies, 1961.

Wain, J. *Essays on Literature and Ideas*. London: Macmillan, 1963.

Williams, R. *Culture and Society*, Part 3, Ch. 6. London: Chatto & Windus, 1958.

————. *Orwell*. London: Fontana Books, 1971.

Willison, I. R. *George Orwell: Some Materials for a Bibliography*. University of London, School of Librarianship and Archives.

Woodcock, G. *The Crystal Spirit*. Boston: Little, Brown, 1966.